Basic
principles
for the
practice
of the
church life

witness lee

Living Stream Ministry
Anaheim, California

First Edition, March 1999.

ISBN 0-7363-0491-6

Published by

Living Stream Ministry
2431 W. La Palma Ave., Anaheim, CA 92801 U.S.A.
P. O. Box 2121, Anaheim, CA 92814 U.S.A.

Printed in the United States of America

99 00 01 02 03 04 / 9 8 7 6 5 4 3 2 1

CONTENTS

PREFACE

This book is composed of messages given by Brother Witness Lee in a training in Altadena, California in the summer of 1963. These messages were not reviewed by the speaker.

CHAPTER ONE

THE CHURCH AS THE ETERNAL PURPOSE AND HIDDEN MYSTERY OF GOD, AND ITS SOURCE, FUNCTION, AND PRACTICE

Scripture Reading: Eph. 3:11, 9; John 3:26-30; 2 Cor. 5:1

Prayer: Lord, we thank You for this time that we can come together to learn something of Yourself. Lord, we do feel that we are not competent to minister before You in such a matter, so we do trust in You for all the need. Lord, we look to You that You would open Your Word to us that we may see from Your Word, through Your Word, and in Your Word something about Yourself and something about Your Body. Lord, do reveal to us the heavenly things that we may have the heavenly vision in these last days. In Your precious name we ask. Amen.

THE ETERNAL PURPOSE OF GOD

The church is a great subject in the Bible. In these few chapters we will be able to see only some practical principles concerning the church without getting into many details.

First, the church is something of God's eternal plan, His eternal purpose. It is something planned by God in His eternal plan, something purposed by God in eternity and for eternity. Ephesians 3:10-11 gives us the scriptural ground to speak of the church as something of God's eternal purpose. Verse 11 says, "According to the eternal purpose which He made in Christ Jesus our Lord." The Greek word for *purpose* means "plan." God has purposed a purpose, He planned a plan, and this purpose, this plan, is called the eternal purpose. In eternity past, before the foundation of this world, before the heavens, the earth, and all things were created,

God made such a purpose for something in the future, in eternity to come. Therefore, it is called the purpose of eternity, the eternal purpose. Moreover, many passages in the New Testament tell us that this purpose was purposed not only in Christ but also for Christ.

Now we must ask what this purpose is. Verse 10 says, "In order that now to the rulers and authorities in the heavenlies the multifarious wisdom of God might be made known through the church." The eternal purpose of God is that He would have a church. In the whole universe only the church is the subject, the center, and the content of God's eternal plan. This should make us very clear that our being saved to be the members of the church is something not only for this present age; it is something purposed, planned, long before the foundation of this world.

In eternity past and for eternity to come, God planned and purposed to have a church in Christ and for Christ. Therefore, the church is not a temporary matter but an eternal matter. The church is in this age and throughout this age, yet it is from eternity past and for eternity future. It is an eternal matter in the eternal purpose of God, and it is the center, the subject of God's eternal plan. God planned in eternity past to have a church, and God expects to have the church in eternity to come.

THE MYSTERY HIDDEN IN GOD

Throughout all the generations before the New Testament time, the church was a mystery. *Mystery* indicates that something was hidden that no one knew about. Do you know why God created the heavens, the earth, and thousands and thousands of items? Do you know why God created the race of Adam, the human people? You need to answer this question by saying, "It was to have the church." The intention, the desire, of God is not to have heaven, not to have the earth, and not to have many different items. The intention, the desire, of God in this universe is to have the church. Therefore, everything is for the church. We may illustrate this with a brother I once met. This brother was busy day by day with so many matters in order to build a house and prepare its furniture. One day I asked him what all these preparations were for. He replied that it was so that his son could have a bride. This is exactly an illustration, a type, of what God did in creation in order for Christ to have a bride. Heaven, earth, and all things created by God are a "new house" for Christ so that He may marry His bride. They are the preparation for Christ to have the church.

The church is the central thought of God's intention, but before the New Testament time God never told anyone about this. In the Old Testament times people looked up to the heavens and could say, "Oh, it is so wonderful." Abraham once looked up to the heavens to count the stars, and the psalmist in Psalm 8 said in the night, "When I see Your heavens, the works of Your fingers, / The moon and the stars, which You have ordained, / What is man, that You remember him, / And the son of man, that You visit him?" (vv. 3-4). However, if we could ask Abraham and the psalmist what the heavens were made for, they would not know. They could only say that the heavens magnify the glory of God. However, please remember that the heavens are not only for the glory of God to be manifested but also as a preparation for Christ to have the church.

The heavens, the earth, and all things are for the church, but before the New Testament time God never told this to anyone. Adam did not know it, Abraham did not know it, Moses did not know it, and David did not know it. It was a mystery; no one in the Old Testament times ever knew it. Is this still a mystery to you today? Before you read this message, you may not have been clear why God created all things, but now it is no longer a mystery

The New Testament tells us that the church was a mystery hidden in God. Ephesians 3:9 says, "And to enlighten all that they may see what the economy of the mystery is, which throughout the ages has been hidden in God, who created all things." From the beginning of the world the purpose of creation was hidden in God as a mystery. All creatures could see that there is a creation, but no one knew what the purpose of it is. One day the Lord came, and He died, resurrected, ascended, came down as the Holy Spirit, and raised up a number of persons. Some of these persons were apostles, prophets, and teachers, who received the revelation. The mystery hidden in God was revealed to them at that time. They saw and came to know that the purpose of creation is to have the church. The church was a mystery hidden in God in the past generations until in the New Testament time it was revealed to the apostles and prophets.

THE NATURE, SOURCE, AND ESSENCE OF THE CHURCH

The first thing we have seen is that the church is something of God's eternal purpose, and the second point is that this purpose was hidden in God as a mystery. Now we must see what the church is. Some may quickly say that the church is the Body of Christ and the house of God. Since the Brethren were raised up by God in 1828, they wrote many books on these two aspects of the church. Whenever you meet the Brethren and talk with them, they may tell you that the church is the Body of Christ and the house of God. From the time of the Brethren until today, nearly all the seeking Christians have come to know this. This is one hundred percent correct, but I wish to speak in a more subjective way. The Body of Christ is subjective, but there is still something more subjective than this. The Body of Christ and the house of God are the function of the church, but these aspects do not show us the nature and the source of the church.

The term that can help us to see the source and the nature of the church is *increase*. The church is the increase of Christ. Therefore, Christ is the source of the church and the nature of the church. The church is something out of Christ; it is Christ Himself increased and enlarged. This term to describe the church is more subjective.

Christ is the very source of the church, and Christ is the very nature, even the very essence, of the church. If a person were to grow one hundred times larger than he is now, he would still be the same person, but in an increased and enlarged way. In the same way, the church is Christ Himself increased and enlarged.

The scriptural support for this is John 3:30. In this verse, John the Baptist speaks of the Son of God, Christ, by saying, "He must increase, but I must decrease." More than thirty years ago I was taught from this verse that in our daily lives Christ must be increased, enlarged to be everything, and we must be decreased, reduced to nothing. I was much helped by such a teaching. In all my daily life by the grace of God I tried to be reduced. "No longer I...but...Christ" (Gal. 2:20) simply means I am reduced and Christ is increased. However, the correct meaning of John 3:30 is not what I was taught.

In these last few years we have received the correct meaning of this verse according to its context. Verse 26 says, "And they came unto John and said to him, Rabbi, He who was with you across the Jordan, of whom you have testified, behold, He is baptizing and all are coming to Him." The disciples of John saw that all men came to the Lord Jesus. They were not happy, so they came to John, their rabbi, and told him about it. Verses 27-29 say, "John answered and said, A man cannot receive anything unless it has been given to him from heaven. You yourselves testify of me that I said, I am not the Christ, but I have been sent before Him. He who has the bride is the bridegroom; but the friend of the bridegroom, who stands and hears him, rejoices with joy because of the bridegroom's voice. This joy of mine therefore is made full." By the context of these verses we may know that all who come to the Lord to be redeemed by Him are the Lord's bride, and the Lord is the Bridegroom. John the Baptist is not this Bridegroom; he is the friend of the Bridegroom. It is the Lord who is the Bridegroom who will have the bride.

Following this, the next verse says, "He must increase." What does this mean? This simply means that Christ will have a bride, and the bride is His increase. In the previous verse there is the bride, and in this verse there is the increase. We should underline these two words, *bride* in verse 29 and *increase* in verse 30. The increase in verse 30 is the bride in verse 29.

We can rightly understand how the bride is the increase by means of the types in the Old Testament. The first type of this kind is Eve as a bride to Adam to be Adam's increase. Eve was the first bride, and this bride was the increase of Adam. Adam was a bachelor, a single person. One day, the Lord God caused this bachelor, this single Adam, to sleep. While he was sleeping, God opened Adam's side, took a rib out of him, and made this rib into a woman as a bride to match this bachelor. This rib became a counterpart to match the single Adam. Now this bachelor was no more single. There was a couple, yet this bride, this wife, was the increase of Adam. Previously Adam was single, but now he had a wife, a counterpart, to match him. Genesis 2 tells us that these two became one flesh. These two were not two persons but one person as two counterparts; the wife was a counterpart of the husband, and the husband was the counterpart to the wife. They two were a complete person, a couple. By this we can see that a wife is the increase of her husband. If we look at a husband and wife today, we may not realize that the wife is something out of the husband. But if we could see Adam and Eve standing together, we would immediately be able to see that Eve was something out of Adam as the increase of Adam.

Eve was formed from a rib of Adam, indicating that the bride is the increase of the bridegroom and comes out of the bridegroom as a part of the bridegroom. Therefore, the church is a "rib" of the last Adam. The church is a part of Christ, something coming out of Christ. One day God caused Christ to sleep on the cross, and while Christ slept there, God opened Christ, and something came out of Christ. John 19:34 says that blood and water came out of His side. The blood is for redeeming, to redeem us from sins, and the water is for life-giving, to impart life to us. By this we become the members of Christ. Corporately speaking, we become the corporate Body of Christ, and this very corporate Body is the bride, the increase of Christ and the counterpart to match Christ. We all must realize what the church is. The church is the increase of Christ.

In the third chapter of the Gospel of John we see the words *bride* and *increase*. Now we must see another word, *regeneration*. We must be regenerated, reborn, by Christ. John 3 is a chapter on regeneration, but for what purpose does God regenerate people? Regeneration is to produce a bride for Christ. It is to produce all the members of the Body of Christ, and the Body of Christ is a bride to match Christ as His increase. Therefore, John 3 speaks of regeneration, the bride, and the increase. How can we be a part, a member, of the bride of Christ? It is by regeneration. Christ has to impart His life into us to make us a part of His bride. Thus by regeneration Christ gains a bride, and this very bride is the increase of Himself.

Ephesians 1:23 says that this increase is the fullness of Christ. The church is the Body of Christ, which is the fullness of the One who fills all in all. Christ is unlimited, so He needs a Body to be His fullness. As the bride the church is the increase of Christ, while as the Body the church is the fullness of the Head. A head without a body is very poor, for it has no fullness. A person's body is the fullness of his head, and a big body is a bigger fullness. The church, which is the Body of Christ, is the fullness of the Head. The bride is the increase of the Husband, and the Body is the fullness of the Head. That the church is the increase of Christ shows us the source, the nature, and the essence of the church. The very source, the very nature, and the very essence of the church are nothing less than Christ Himself because the church is one hundred percent out of Christ and a part of Christ. It is Christ Himself increased and enlarged.

Now we know why God created the heavens, the earth, so many items, and the human race. It was simply for Christ to come into His creation, to be incarnated into the human race, to impart Himself to the human race, in order to make a part of the human race a part of Himself. Without the heavens, the earth, and so many items it would not be possible for the human race to exist, and without the existence of the human race it would be impossible for Christ to be increased. In order to have a human race for Christ to be increased, there is the need of the universe as an environment in which and by which the human race can exist. If the sun in the heavens were only a little farther from the earth, we would die from the cold, and if the sun were a little nearer, we all would be burned. But now the temperature on the earth is just right to fit the purpose that we may live. In addition, all the vitamins in the animal and vegetable lives were intended by God for man to exist. If we study the universe with such a point of view, we will be very happy and see that the entire universe was made and arranged by God for the purpose that the human race may exist so that Christ may come to be incarnated, to become a man, to impart Himself to the human race, to make a part of the human race a bride for Himself as His increase. Now we can see the central position that the church has in this universe. The universe is for the human race, the human race is for the church, and the church is the increase of Christ.

THE FUNCTION OF THE CHURCH

The fourth point we must see is the function of the church. Now we may come back to the Body of Christ and the house of God. To Christ the church is a Body; Christ is the Head and the church is the Body. To God the church is a house; God is the Resident and the church is the residence. In principle the Body and the house are the same. In the New Testament our body is likened to a house. Second Corinthians 5:1 says that our body is a house, a dwelling place. The Body is a container to contain the life of the Head, and the house is also a container, a residence, to contain the One who dwells in the house. The Body is a vessel and the house is also a vessel. Where is Christ contained? In the Body. Where is God contained; that is, where does He dwell? In His house. In principle, to speak of the Body or the house is the same because both the house and the Body are containers, vessels, to contain God and Christ.

However, there is still a difference. The Body as a container is to express the life which it contains. Therefore, with the Body there is the aspect of expression. All that we are, all we can do, and all we have are expressed through our body. It is by means of a person's body that he can speak, walk, demonstrate his wisdom and knowledge, and do many things. The body is a container to express what it contains. However, the main point of a house is not to express something. With a house the main point is rest, completion, and accomplishment. To accomplish something, we need a house. In these days we are endeavoring to publish a little magazine entitled *The Stream,* and we will now publish some more messages in booklet form. For this we need a room in a house. A house is for resting and for the completing of a purpose. Christ needs the church as a Body to express Himself, while God needs the church as a house to rest and to do His will, to accomplish His eternal purpose.

Now we know what the source, the nature, and the essence of the church are and what the function of the church is. To Christ it is a Body; it contains Christ to express Christ. To God it is a house; it contains God for God to rest in it and to accomplish His will through it. This is the function, the duty, of the church.

THE PRACTICE OF THE CHURCH

Now we may see a practical point, the practice of the church. How the church is practiced is a great issue for the believers. First we must realize that the church was formed and founded universally, the church is built up universally, and the church is practiced universally, in the whole universe, and among the human race. From the time of Pentecost the Lord began to establish His church, to practice His church, not only in one place, in one locality, but in many places, in many localities, in locality after locality and place after place. Moreover, this was not only in one age or generation but in age after age and generation after generation.

We all know the meaning of the word *universal*. It refers to time plus space, what is throughout all time and throughout all space. Localities are a matter of space, generations are a matter of time, and space plus time equals the universe. Therefore, the Lord formed, founded, establishes, builds up, and practices His church universally. In place after place, time after time, city after city, nation after nation, and generation after generation the Lord practices the church universally.

However, while the Lord practices the church universally, there is still the local aspect. I must ask you to be very sober-minded in this matter because today in Christianity there are some wrong speakings, saying that there are two different kinds of churches, one being the eternal and universal church and the other being the local churches. We must say no to this. This is a wrong speaking. We can only speak of different aspects of the church, not different kinds of churches.

The local churches comprise the universal church, and the one universal church is the local churches. We may illustrate this with our human body, which is one whole with many members. The body is the members, and the many members are the body. They are not two things but exactly one thing in two different aspects. If we look at it as a whole, it is a body, but if we look at it as the parts, there are many, yet the parts are still one body. Can we separate our body from its members? This is ridiculous. However, I am sorry to say that even today some people preach and teach that the universal church is something other than the local churches.

It is impossible to separate the universal church from the local churches. Without the local churches where is the universal church? This is like asking where a body is apart from its members. If we do not have the church in Jerusalem, the church in Antioch, the church in London, New York, San Francisco, or Los Angeles, or the local churches in Taiwan and Japan, where is the universal church? The universal church is a composition of all the local churches, and all the local churches are just part after part of the one universal church. All the local churches throughout the generations and in all the places are the members composed together as one universal church. We should not have the thought that the universal church is something other than the local churches. This is an error, a wrong teaching, and a kind of heresy.

Today especially, we hear many people talking about the universal church, but where is the universal church? I have been studying this matter for more than thirty years, and up to today I cannot say where the universal church is if it is apart from the local churches. I would challenge someone to point to where the universal church is. On the other hand, I can point to where the local churches are. Nineteen hundred years ago there was one in Jerusalem, one in Samaria, one in Antioch, one in Corinth, one in Ephesus, and another one in Rome. Today there is one in Los Angeles and another one in New York. I can point to many local churches, but can someone point to where the universal church is? The universal church is so great, but we cannot point to it. We must not blindly follow those wrong and foolish teachings.

Where the local churches are, there the universal church is. We cannot say that besides the members there is a body. Rather, we must say that a body is with the members, not in addition to the members. By this we can see what the universal church is. The universal church is the totality, the ultimate consummation, of the composition of all the local churches.

We may use the term *the universal church,* but its proper use depends on what kind of interpretation we have. The universal church is an issue of all the local churches throughout all the generations and throughout all the places. All these local churches throughout all the generations and places, added and composed together as one, are called the universal church. Without the local churches and besides the local churches, there is no universal church.

Let us be clear about this. Eventually, we will see who is right and who is wrong in this matter. The Bible shows us and reveals to us that in this universe there is only one church, which is the Body of Christ expressed in many parts in many places throughout all the generations. A part of this Body was expressed nineteen hundred years ago in Jerusalem. Another part was expressed at the same time in Antioch, and today a part is expressed in our own locality. In one aspect, the church is universal, and in the other aspect, it is local. It is universal as a whole and local in its parts, and all these parts added together and composed as one, are the Body of Christ.

Therefore, the church is practiced universally by being practiced locally. Without the local practice there is no possibility of the universal practice. Where is the practice of the universal church? Is it on the moon, in the third heavens, or in Paradise? We cannot find such a thing in the entire universe. Strictly speaking, there is no universal practice of the church; there is only the local practice. Since the day of Pentecost all the local practices of the church added together and composed together as one are corporately called the universal practice. What is the universal practice of the church? It is the composition of all the local practices.

I simply cannot tolerate to hear so many of the Lord's servants preach foolishly, telling people that besides the local churches there is a universal church. I would ask where, besides the local churches, is the universal church? We can never touch it. The practice of the church, strictly speaking, is local. Without the local church we can never have the universal church, and without the local practices we can never have a universal practice of the church. In the New Testament there are twenty-seven books, including the twenty-one Epistles plus the seven epistles in Revelation 2 and 3. Which Epistle was addressed to the universal church? At most, an Epistle may say that it should be read by other churches. First Corinthians, for example, was meant for the Corinthians as well as for all the believers in every place. However, it was not addressed to the universal church. We must be clear about this and concentrate all our attention on the local expressions of the church.

Chapter Two

THE EXPRESSION, CONTENT, AND ORDER OF THE CHURCH

Scripture Reading: Acts 1:8; Phil. 1:1; Acts 20:28; 1 Pet. 5:5-6

In the previous chapter we saw five points concerning the church. The church is something of God's eternal purpose, something planned, purposed, by God in eternity past and for eternity to come. Therefore, the church is something eternal. If we have the revelation from the Word of God, we will realize that the church is the center of God's eternal purpose. What God purposed in eternity past and for eternity to come is to have a church as the center of His purpose. Thus, the church is a central and eternal matter. Second, we saw that in the Old Testament time the church was a mystery hidden in God. Before the New Testament time the church was in the mind of God, but God never revealed it to anyone. Third, we saw the source of the church. The source of the church is Christ Himself, the Son of God. The church is something out of Christ Himself and a part of Christ Himself as His increase and as a counterpart to match Him. By this we can see that Christ is the nature of the church. Fourth, we saw the functions of the church. On one hand, it is a Body to Christ, and on the other hand, it is a house to God. These are the two aspects of the function of the church. Fifth, we saw clearly that the practice of the church, strictly speaking, can never be universal. It must be local. The universal practice is all the practices of the churches in their localities added together. Without or besides the local practices, we can never have the universal practice of the church.

THE EXPRESSION OF THE CHURCH

In this chapter we shall consider some further points

concerning the church. The sixth point is the expression of the church. This seems very close to the practice of the church, yet there is a difference. The church is something real and is very substantial; it is not something "in the air" or merely a theory in our mind. It is something composed of all the redeemed believers in the New Testament time built together with the Triune God. Therefore, it is very real and substantial, so there must be an expression of this real and substantial matter.

The church is expressed on this earth. It is absolutely wrong to think that the church is something expressed in heaven. There is no verse in the Scriptures to support this wrong idea. The church is not expressed in heaven, but on the earth. I have spent much time to study the New Testament to find out whether there is something of the church in heaven. I speak the truth: I cannot find such a thing. Is there a verse in the twenty-eight chapters of Matthew, for example, to prove that the church today is in heaven? Is there such a word concerning the church in Mark, Luke, John, Acts, or the Epistles? First Thessalonians 4:17 says that we shall meet the Lord in the air, but that will be at the Lord's coming. By this verse we cannot prove that the church is in heaven today.

The church is heavenly, but the church is not in heaven. Many of the saints, including Abraham, David, and Paul, are in Paradise, but none of them are in heaven. In his reference Bible, Dr. C. I. Scofield says that Paradise, where the saved ones are, was translated from the pleasant part of Hades to the third heavens when the Lord was resurrected and ascended to heaven. However, in Acts 2:34, when Peter stood up to speak on the day of Pentecost, he said that David had not ascended into heaven. The spirits and souls of all the dead saints, both from the Old Testament time and the New Testament time, are in Paradise and not in heaven. Therefore, we cannot find a verse to prove that the church today is in heaven.

The expression of the church is one hundred percent upon this earth in localities, in one place after another. The first expression of the church was in Jerusalem, in a locality, a city, a place on this earth. After that, there were many expressions in Judea and Samaria. Then the expression of the church expanded to Antioch, and it turned to the west, to many cities in Asia Minor. In each city there was an expression of the church. There was one in Ephesus, one in Smyrna, one in Pergamos, one in Thyatira, one in Sardis, one in Philadelphia, and one in Laodicea. In each city there was an expression of the church. If we follow the record of the Acts and the Epistles, we will find that the church is something expressed on this earth in place after place, in city after city.

Built Up with Redeemed Persons on the Earth

Why did God make the church to be expressed in such a way? There are several reasons. First, the church must be built up with redeemed persons, and the redeemed persons, even after they have been redeemed, are still on this earth, living in human communities and in human society. The redeemed persons have not been taken away to the heavens. The church is a composition of saved and redeemed ones set free and separated from the satanic, evil system of the world, the system on the earth, yet still remaining on this earth and living among humans. Therefore, the church must be expressed on this earth in the human community and society. It is impossible for the church to be built up where there are no materials for the church. In a desert where there are no humans, there can never be an expression of the church. We must come to a city within human society to gain the materials from human society for the building up of the church.

There is the need for the church to be expressed upon this earth and among people in society. This does not mean that the church belongs to this world. To be in this world is one thing, while to belong to this world is another thing. To be separated from the world does not mean to leave the world. We do not belong to the satanic system of this world, and we are separated from it, yet we still remain here and live here. The church is expressed on this earth among human society in order that the church can gain some materials, who are delivered, saved, and separated out of human society. This is one reason why the church must be expressed on earth. Do not send the church to the heavens. We must keep the church in our locality and in all the cities on this earth.

Having the Great Commission of the Gospel

Second, the Lord has committed the church with a mission. The great commission committed to the church by the Lord is that the church must bring the Lord as the gospel to human beings. The church must be expressed among people in order to preach the gospel to people. We have this responsibility and obligation, and we have been committed with this mission. It is a great mission, and it is nearly the unique mission. We have been committed to preach Christ as the gospel to people, so the church must be expressed among people on this earth.

To Express Christ as Life among Humanity

Third, Christ as life to us must also be expressed among humanity. We do not express Christ merely to the angels; we have to express Christ among the human beings on the earth. Therefore, the church must be expressed on this earth in the localities where people are gathered and centered. Wherever there is a center, a gathering of people, there must be the expression of the church.

To Accomplish
God's Eternal Purpose on the Earth

Fourth, God has His eternal purpose, and He must do something to accomplish His purpose on this earth through the church. Therefore, the church must exist on this earth among humans to carry out the eternal purpose of God.

The church is heavenly, but it must be expressed on the earth. We may not realize how much damage is done when people say, "Since the church is heavenly, it must be carried out in heaven." When I was young, I was taught that all the so-called churches on this earth are not real and that the real church will be in heaven; all the visible churches are not the real churches because the real church is the invisible church. However, I do not know where there is an invisible church in this universe. We cannot find such a church. The church is something heavenly, yet it must be expressed on this earth. In the record of the Acts and the Epistles, the apostles stressed that the church must be local. We can find the church in Jerusalem, the church in Antioch, the church in Samaria, and the church in Ephesus; we can find many churches on the earth, but we can never find a church in the heavens. The church must be expressed on this earth.

The Expression of the Church
Being One in Every Locality

Moreover, as the church is expressed on this earth, that expression must be one. In every city, in every locality where people are gathered together, there must be an expression of the church, and that expression must be only one. It can never be and should never be more than one. In Jerusalem the expression of the church was one, in Antioch the expression of the church was one, and in Ephesus the expression of the church was one. We cannot find a case in the Scriptures where in a certain city there was more than one expression. This is simply because the church is one. The church is expressed on this earth in localities where people are gathered, and wherever there is an expression of the church in a locality, it must be one. When I was in New York, someone asked me what we should do with a church in a city that has millions of people. I turned the question to the one who asked it and said, "How many governments do you have in New York, and how many city halls do you have? Can you have more than one city hall in New York? Can you have two city halls? It is impossible." To have two city halls in New York because it is so big means that we divide the one New York City into two cities.

We may think that in a city with a population of several million it is impossible for us to have one church. However, human society can have one city hall in a city with more than ten million people. To have one church in a city, there is no need for all the people to meet together in one meeting place. In a family of five persons it is not necessary to have all five persons in one room. One family may use many rooms, and the members of a family may even live in different apartments. A large family with a grandfather, grandmother, husband, wife, and many children and grandchildren may live in a large compound with several buildings. However, they are still one family. There is no need to meet in one place in order to be one church. We can have many meetings in a big city, but all the saints who meet in different places are still one church. Acts 2 and 4 say that at the time of the apostles the church in Jerusalem met in houses, from house to house. They had many separate meetings, but they were still one church. According to the first eight chapters of Acts, the saints in Jerusalem met in houses separately, but they were still called the one church in Jerusalem (8:1).

Large numbers are not a problem. On one day the apostles baptized three thousand people, and on another day five thousand were saved and baptized. They were able to do this because they had been trained while the Lord was on the earth. When the Lord fed the five thousand with five loaves and two fish, He trained the disciples. He did not pray and bless the loaves and then distribute them in a messy way to let the people fight over them. Rather, the Lord told the disciples to have the crowd sit in groups, by hundreds and by fifties. When people sit down, they are quiet and in order. This illustrates that to care for many people is easy. For the one hundred twenty disciples in Acts to take care of three thousand or five thousand on one day was not very difficult. We have had this experience. On one day in only two hours we baptized seven hundred people.

We need to realize that the church must be expressed on the earth in the localities where people are gathered. Moreover, each expression of the church, no matter where it is, must be one. There is no reason for us to be divided. If we go to London, there must be one church there; we belong to the church, so we meet with the church. We should not ask people there what kind of church they have, just as we cannot ask them what kind of moon they have. The moon is just one. In the same way, there is only one church. When I go to Los Angeles, I meet with the church there. Likewise, when I go to New York, San Francisco, Tokyo, or Hong Kong, I meet with the church there. There is no reason for us to be divided. We are members of the church. Wherever we go, we simply meet with the church. This is the proper way ordained by the Lord.

God ordained the church to be expressed in a very simple way. Where there is a gathering of people in a locality, we have to preach the gospel to them. Then some of them will be separated by the Lord's salvation, and these separated ones need to come together as the expression of the church in that community, in that locality. The church is expressed on this earth in localities, and where there is an expression of the church, that expression must be one. Let us be simple. Let us not be complicated by the confusion in Christianity. It is a shame to ask people what church they belong to. If someone is a brother, that is all we need to know. I belong to the church, and you belong to the church. We all belong to the church.

More than thirty-two years ago, when we were in Shanghai, three or four brothers rode on a street car to go to the meeting, each with a Bible in his hand. Another believer, who was distributing tracts to the riders on the car, came to them and realized that they were brothers. That brother asked them, "To what church do you belong?" The three or four brothers looked at one another and wondered how to answer. Then one of the oldest among them told him, "We belong to the church to which you, Paul, Peter, Martin Luther, and all the saints belong." After considering this, the brother with the tracts said, "This is wonderful!" To be sure, it is wonderful. To tell people that we belong to a certain kind of church is not glorious. We are nothing; we are only the general members of the one church. That is all.

THE CONTENT OF THE CHURCH

The seventh point which we will consider is the content of the church. We must remember well that the content of the church cannot be and should not be anything other than the Lord Christ Himself. The church is a container to contain Christ, not anything else. Only the Lord Christ is the content of the church. If we realize this well and keep this well in mind and in spirit, that would be wonderful. The church is the Body of Christ. A body is a container, a vessel, to contain the life of the head. In the same way, the church is the container to contain Christ. We may have teachings, gifts, and knowledge, but all these teachings, gifts, and knowledge must be a help to people that they may realize Christ more and more. As long as we encounter any kind of teaching, any kind of gift, or any kind of knowledge that detaches people from Christ, we must depreciate it because the content of the church is Christ Himself. We can use many means, including teachings, gifts, and knowledge, to bring people to Christ, to help people, to prompt people, even to urge people to Christ, but we must realize that nothing can be a substitute for Christ.

I do not like to say something to criticize anyone or any Christian organizations, but certain groups of Christians have certain systems, which apparently are their contents. Some groups of believers have certain doctrines, and other groups of Christians have certain gifts. We must be clear that all the doctrines, gifts, and knowledge are good as long as they help people to realize Christ and do not take people away from Christ. We need to realize very clearly that the church is a corporate vessel as a container to contain Christ, and Christ is the very content of the church.

When we come together, what do we express? We need to express Christ, either by prayer, by work, by a hymn, by a testimony, or by a teaching. What we have must be an expression of Christ. If we have something else as a center, we are sectarian. We often say that we have to be general Christians. Do you know what a general Christian is? A general Christian is a person general with Christ and with nothing else. We are so general with Christ. We have Christ and nothing else as the center. We can keep everything, or we can lay everything aside. If this everything is a help to take Christ as the center, we keep it. If this everything is a damage, a hindrance, to have Christ as the center, we set it aside. We should not insist on anything but Christ.

In the Christian meeting I attended when I was young, I was taught that a man should not have long hair but should cut his hair very short. People there were also taught not to wear leather shoes but to wear the old style of Chinese shoes, and the sisters were taught not to wear certain kinds of dresses. If one of us today were to go there, they might tell us not to come back until we cut our hair and change our shoes. These people studied the Scriptures daily, taught the Scriptures, and were very strict. I was with them for quite a period of time, but later I realized that their strictness was not Christ.

If you travel over the whole world, you will see how many different kinds of Christian churches there are, with many different kinds of peculiar emphases. Many groups stress certain things other than Christ. Recently I traveled along the west coast of the United States. Wherever I went, I often met some Pentecostal saints who asked me, "Do you speak in tongues? What about speaking in tongues?" I do not oppose speaking in tongues, but I must tell the Lord's children that if we insist too much on speaking in tongues, we are sectarian. If we classify ourselves as "Spirit-filled persons" in a "Spirit-filled church," we are sectarian. This is to make ourselves too special. We should not make ourselves special among the Lord's children. We are general children of God. I believe in speaking in tongues in the right way, but I cannot believe that all the so-called tongues throughout the world today are the genuine ones. Perhaps only a small percent are genuine. Nevertheless, we should not insist even on the genuine speaking in tongues.

I have had many talks with the saints in the Far East and in the west, including Europe, about this matter. I pointed out to those dear ones who insist on speaking in tongues that many spiritual, powerful, and prevailing persons in the past never spoke in tongues. Brother Hudson Taylor, the founder of the China Inland Mission, was a very powerful and spiritual man. We can even say that he was a spiritual giant, but he never spoke in tongues. George Müller was also a very spiritual man in the last century, but he never spoke in tongues. I do not oppose speaking in tongues, but you must realize that it is not our center. It is not something that is everything to us.

We should insist on nothing but Christ being everything to us. I agree that we must have baptism by immersion in water, but I do not insist on it. If some brothers or sisters do not agree with it, we can still go along with them. We must be careful not to insist on anything other than Christ. Christ is the center, and Christ is the everything of the church. If anything helps people to realize Christ, let us take it. If it is not helpful, let us drop it. We may keep all things, and we may lay all things aside, but we insist on Christ as the center and as everything. Christ is the content of the church.

THE ORDER OF THE CHURCH

The eighth point concerning the church is the order of the church. Philippians 1:1 says, "Paul and Timothy, slaves of Christ Jesus, to all the saints in Christ Jesus who are in Philippi, with the overseers and deacons." This verse speaks of the saints with the overseers and deacons. This refers to the order of the church. As a group of the Lord's children coming together to realize the church life, to have the expression of the Body, the church, we have a real need of a spiritual order. I do not like to use the word *organization;* this is something wrong. But according to the teaching of the Scriptures, there must be a spiritual order among the saints. According to Acts 20, the overseers are the elders. An overseer is someone who oversees the situation in the church. In the churches there are always some leading ones. The elders are the ones who take the responsibility to care for the church, and the deacons are the ones who serve the church.

We all need much grace to keep the right order among the Lord's children. To keep the order we must have elders. A brother needs much grace to be an elder. There are very many needs in the church. To be an elder, a person has to be broken, broad-minded, full of Christ, humble in the spirit, and patient in the spirit. He must also have some amount of spiritual knowledge, and he must be filled with God as love and saturated by the Spirit as wisdom. Oh, how much grace one needs to be an elder! As we have seen, he first must be broken and humble. If one has never been humble, he can never be an elder.

Not only so, we also need much grace to submit to the elders. There is the need to be the elders, and there is the need to submit to the elders. The first time I went to Shanghai thirty years ago, I encountered two brothers. The first brother came to the church in Shanghai first, and after a certain time, the second brother was brought in through the first brother. However, after a certain period of time, the second brother had improved, grown, and matured much in the Lord, while the first brother remained as a child and still spoke as a child. When it came time for the church to establish elders, the second brother was established as an elder, and the first one was not. From that time onward, the first brother complained and asked why the second had become an elder, and he, the first, had not. He could never submit himself to the second brother. I speak frankly; to submit yourself to someone else requires much grace, sometimes even more grace.

First Corinthians 11 tells us that God is the head of Christ, Christ is the head of every man, and man is the head of the woman (v. 3). Therefore, the woman must be covered (vv. 5-6). Man is the head, and the woman has to be covered. For man to be the head requires much grace. If one does not have the grace, it is impossible for him to be the head. I have experienced this. To be a head is not simple. In the years that I was in Shanghai, many times I told the Lord, "I almost long to be a sister." How nice it is to be a sister because to be a brother, as the head, one has to take care of many things. He must be suppressed and put down, and he must learn the lessons to be broken, to be humble, and to be patient. Oh, there are so many lessons! Eventually all the burdens will come to him.

One day, the main one among the leading sisters came to me about a certain matter and said, "Brother Lee, in this matter you brothers must take the responsibility." I said, "Yes, sister, there is no doubt about this." She said, "Good. Let us sisters go in peace." I said, "Sister, you can go in peace, while we bear the burden." After that I told the Lord, "Lord, I long to be a sister so that I could go in peace." Brothers, do you realize that you are brothers and that you must take care of the burdens? You cannot go in peace. How easy and comfortable it is to be a sister. This illustrates that to be an elder in the real church life is not an easy matter. It requires much grace.

Nevertheless, I realize that if I were a sister, it would not be easy to submit myself to the brothers. One day a sister came to me and said, "Brother Lee, I know we sisters have to submit to you brothers as the head, but you brothers must know what kind of head you need to be. We sisters can submit to a certain kind of head, but we cannot submit ourselves to any kind of head. A human has a head, but so does a hammer and an axe." That sister challenged me, asking, "Brother Lee, what kind of head are you brothers going to be? The head of a hammer, hammering us all the time?" This shows that it is not easy to submit to others. Especially today in the twentieth century, throughout the whole world the human race is inclining toward independence. Everyone wants to be independent. Even the children want to be independent of their parents, and the students want to be independent of their teachers and school. No one wants to submit to another, but if there is no submission, how can there be an order? How can there be the real Body life?

A certain brother has three grandchildren, the youngest of whom is about two years old. One day I said to her, "Baby, how are you?" She said, "I am not a baby! I am big!" Even such a small girl wants to be big in her family. It is human nature to want to be big. On the way to Jerusalem as the Lord was going to be crucified, the disciples argued about who was the greatest. Was there the possibility of an order being built up among them?

We say that we are going to have the church life, but what about submission? It is not easy to submit ourselves to others. I can never forget how thirty years ago Brother Watchman Nee said in a message, "To submit yourself to others requires more grace." He used the words *more grace*. We need more grace to submit ourselves to others. Not only do the brothers and sisters need to submit to the elders, but even the elders need to learn the lesson to submit themselves to all the brothers. We need to learn the lesson to submit to one another. This is taught in 1 Peter 5, which implies that even the elders should submit themselves to the younger ones (v. 5).

We need to submit to one another so that there will be a nice, wonderful, spiritual order among us. This order is the real church life, and this order is the real building up of the church. We say that we want to have the church life and the building up of the church, but we must realize that the real church life and the real building up of the church is a spiritual order. For this, we all need grace. Each one of us needs grace to keep our position and stand where we ought to stand. Each one needs the grace to keep his own position so that we can have a spiritual order among us. Then we will realize the real church life. If we do not have the order, it is impossible to have the church life.

What we have spoken here is something truly profitable. We need to realize that the church is expressed on the earth in the localities where people are gathered, and wherever we go we must keep in mind that there is one church, one expression of the Body of Christ. We must respect and honor this principle. Moreover, we must realize that the content of the church is Christ Himself, and we must learn the lesson by grace to keep our own position so that the order of the church may be kept and maintained, so that we may have the real church life. The expression of the church, the content of the church, and the order of the church are the three most practical matters in the church life. May the Lord grant us the grace to see these matters and to keep them.

CHAPTER THREE

THE AUTHORITY IN THE CHURCH

Scripture Reading: Eph. 5:22-25; Gal. 3:27-28; 1 Cor. 12:12-13

In the previous chapters we saw that the church is the central thought, the center, of God's eternal purpose. Before the New Testament time, it was never revealed to anyone but was hidden as a mystery in God, who created the universe. The source of the church is Christ, so the church is the increase of Christ. The function of the church is to be the Body of Christ and the house of God. Moreover, the practice of the church is local, not universal, it is expressed in localities, its content is Christ, and it has a proper order.

The proper order of the church is seen in Philippians 1:1, which speaks of the saints, the overseers, who are the elders, and the deacons. In the church we have the saints as the basic members, and among the saints we have elders and deacons. On the one hand, we realize that in the church there is no human organization, but on the other hand, the Scriptures tell us clearly that there is an order in the church. Not only from the teachings of the Scriptures, but also from our experience we can see that without this order under the Holy Spirit there is no possibility to have the real church life, the real practice of the church. The real church practice depends very much on this order under the Holy Spirit.

In this chapter we come to the ninth point concerning the church, the authority in the church. The order of the church comes out of the authority in the church. We should consider in detail what the authority in the church is. We are told clearly that the church is the Body of Christ and the house of God. To be sure, there is authority in our body, and there is also authority in a house, that is, in a family. Without authority, our house would be a mess. Likewise, as long as a body is living and standing, there is authority in it, but when it becomes a carcass and no longer a body, there is no more authority in it. As long as there is a body there must be authority, and as long as we have a family, a home, there also must be authority. This illustrates that in the church there truly is an authority.

THE HEADSHIP AND LORDSHIP OF CHRIST

The authority of a body is the head. When a person is standing, does his body bear his head, or does his head hold up his body? If we were to cut off a man's head, his body would fall down. Without the head, the body cannot stand. It seems that the body bears the head, but in actuality, it is the head that holds up the body. Therefore, the head is the authority. The Head of the church is Christ the Lord, and the authority in the church is the headship of Christ. It is clear that in the church there should be an order, but this order comes from the headship of Christ. We must realize, honor, and respect the headship of the Lord. If we are not under the headship of the Lord, we can never be right in the order of the church. Many times in the past years, brothers or sisters have come to me and said, "Brother Lee, I simply cannot go along with some of the elders." Every time someone has brought a problem like this to me, I ask them, "At this moment and concerning this very issue, are you under the headship of the Lord?" Invariably, the one asking admits that he or she is not under His headship. I reply, "First you must be right with the Lord. Submit yourself to the headship of the Lord, and then you will be clear."

When I came to the West, to America and Europe, many friends said to me, "People in the Far East are more submissive, while we in the West are more independent. It is probably easy for the brothers and sisters in the Far East to practice the order in the church." However, you should not appreciate the Orientals too much. It is very difficult to deal with the Japanese and the Chinese. I am neither for or against the Orientals or those from the West. All the Orientals and all the Westerners are the descendants of Adam.

There is no difference between us for we are all Adam's race. It is not a matter of East or West. It is a matter of whether or not we are under the headship of Christ and whether or not we have learned the lesson to submit ourselves to the headship of the Lord. In order to keep a right order in the church and among the saints, we must be under the lordship and headship of the Lord. The authority in the church is the headship of the Lord.

PRACTICING THE CHURCH LIFE
BY SUBMITTING TO THE HEADSHIP OF THE LORD

Sometimes elders have come to me, saying, "I simply cannot understand how to be an elder, so I want to resign from the eldership." I have answered such brothers according to the same principle, asking, "Do you feel that at this very moment you are under the headship of the Lord? There is only one way to be an elder, and that is to submit to the headship of the Lord. The more you submit yourself to the headship of the Lord, the more you are qualified and equipped to be an elder."

Once when I delivered a message about the headship, I illustrated it with the need to have an order between a husband and a wife. The husband is the head, and the wife is the one who must submit. That message was very much under the anointing, and a certain brother who heard it was very moved. He regretted that in the past he had not been the proper head in the family, so he prayed, "Lord, help me from today on to be the head." After the meeting he went home and told his wife, "From this time on, I am the head," and he began to practice being the head day by day. Not long after this, trouble came because his wife could not tolerate it. She came to me and asked, "Brother Lee, what kind of a head are the brothers? I simply cannot submit myself to this kind of head." Eventually I learned that neither of this couple was under the headship of Christ. The husband was not, and neither was the wife. There was no real headship, so there was no order. I asked the brother, "While you are assuming the headship, are you under the headship of the Lord?" It is wrong for us to practice any kind of authority if we are not under the headship of the Lord.

Ephesians 5 tells the wives to submit to their husbands, but it tells the husbands to love their wives, not to rule over them. The elders should care for the saints in the same principle. In 1934 I was very young, but since Brother Watchman Nee was absent for a long time, the Lord put the responsibility of the church and the work in Shanghai into my hand. One day the elders came to me and told me about some problems related to the brothers and sisters. I realized that these elders were trying to exercise their authority as elders and were neglecting to show love to the saints. I brought this matter to the Lord. While I was before the Lord one day, the Lord revealed to me in His Word that the husband is the head, but the husband is told not to rule the wife but to love her. The elders have the authority, but they should not exercise their authority. Rather, they should exercise love toward all and extend love to others. This is simply to submit themselves under the headship of the Lord.

The headship of the Lord is the authority in the church. If we want to practice the church life, we have to learn the lesson of always submitting ourselves to the headship of the Lord. The Lord is the Head, and we are all members under His headship. If our relationship is wrong with the Head, we will be wrong with the Body, and to be sure, we will be wrong with the other members. It is when we are right with the Head that we are right with all the members and with the Body. If we are not under the headship, we have no ground to say anything to the brothers and sisters in an adjusting way. If we want to say something to them, we must submit ourselves under the headship of the Lord. To not submit to the headship of the Lord and yet say something to the brothers and sisters simply means that we are rebellious. We are rebellious to the Lord and rebellious to the Body, the church. Please do not think that it is easier to deal with the churches in the Far East than with those in the West. I emphatically say that it is not. Many times certain ones in the Far East came to us to speak about the church in a rebellious way.

We must realize that if we are going to practice the real church life, we must submit ourselves under the headship of Christ. When we are about to say something to the brothers and sisters, we must first test and check whether we are currently under the headship of Christ. If we are not, we should stop. If we are not under the headship, and we say something about the church, we are speaking in a rebellious way. No matter how nice our attitude is, it is false and hypocritical. Our real need is to submit ourselves under the headship of Christ. If we are under the headship of Christ, we will have a pure motive and a right attitude, even if we speak very frankly. But if we are not under the headship of Christ and simply pretend to be nice, we are being political; we are playing politics among the saints.

We must be sincere, open, and frank. Of course, we must also be polite and nice, but we should not pretend. A person who is under the headship of Christ is true, real, and sincere. We may open our heart to a brother to speak something in a serious and frank way, even with heavy words, but if we are submitting ourselves under the headship of the Lord, the Holy Spirit within his spirit can testify for us that our motive is pure and our attitude is right. But on the contrary, if we are not under the headship of the Lord and come to a brother, pretending that we are so good and spiritual, we are playing politics and are a hypocrite among the saints. In this case, the Holy Spirit cannot testify for us. The church has been constantly damaged by these political maneuvers. We must have no political maneuvers. All of us, especially the leading ones, must submit ourselves under the headship.

When the people of Israel rebelled, Moses and Aaron did not play politics and they did not maneuver. They simply knelt and bowed down before the Lord, taking the Lord as the Head, realizing His headship, and letting Him come in. What they said after that, they said in a frank, open, and straight way. This is the right way to realize the headship, the lordship, of Christ as the authority in the church. We do not have a pope among us as the Catholic Church does, to whom all the saints must submit. To exercise authority in this way is devilish; it is from Hades and not from the New Jerusalem. Rather, we all must realize the headship of Christ. The best way to glorify Christ and honor the Lord is to take Him as the Head, praying, "Lord, You are the Head. I take You as the Head, and I speak and act in a genuine way. I am under Your headship."

It is not only the younger ones among us who must submit to Christ and remain under the headship of Christ. Even the oldest ones must submit themselves under the headship of Christ. In the church, if we all realize the headship of Christ, there will spontaneously be a wonderful, spiritual order among us. There will be a situation in which each one knows where he stands and what is his right position in the order of the church. If in a family with many members, all the members are real, sound, spiritual Christians, realizing and submitting to the headship of Christ in their home, there will be a nice, spiritual order in their family. In such a family, even the youngest one will know what his position and standing is, and each one will be right with the order of the family. It is when no one in the family takes the headship of Christ that they fight and quarrel with one another. Then, even the least desires to be the greatest, and the last desires to be the first. There is disorder in such a family simply because they are not under the headship of the Lord.

THE PROBLEM OF BROTHERS AND SISTERS IN THE CHURCH

In the church there are both brothers and sisters. In many places, especially today, the sisters are not willing to submit to the brothers. Some sisters have come to me, saying, "Are not the sisters equal to the brothers? Is there no equality between us? Do you believe that the brothers are greater?" I have even met brothers who stand for the sisters. They say, "We do not agree that we brothers are above the sisters. We are all human. Why do we have to be different from the sisters?"

Galatians 3:27-28 says, "For as many as were baptized into Christ have put on Christ. There cannot be Jew nor Greek, there cannot be slave nor free man, there cannot be male and female; for you are all one in Christ Jesus." *Cannot be Jew nor Greek* indicates that in Christ the problem of races has been dealt with; *cannot be slave nor free man* means that in Christ the problem of social ranks has been dealt with; and *cannot be male and female* indicates that in Christ the problem of gender has been dealt with. However, 1 Corinthians 12:12-13 says, "For even as the body is one and has many members, yet all the members of the body, being many, are one body, so also is the Christ. For also in one Spirit we were all baptized into one body, whether Jews or Greeks, whether slaves or free, and were all given to drink one Spirit." Galatians 3 says we have been baptized into Christ, while 1 Corinthians 12 says we have been baptized into the one Body. However, 1 Corinthians 12 does not mention male and female. In Christ, the problem of male and female has been done away with, but in the church there is still male and female. If there were not the problem of male and female, there would be no need to speak about head covering in the previous chapter, chapter eleven, and there would be no need to speak about the position of sisters in the church meeting in chapter fourteen.

In Christ, the racial problem, the social problem, and the gender problem are all gone. But in the church, while the racial problem and social problem are gone, the problem of male and female still remains. Therefore, when sisters or brothers come to ask why there is a difference between the brothers and sisters, or whether we feel the sisters should submit to the brothers, the only reply is to ask, "Do you take the headship of Christ? Do you submit yourself to the headship of Christ?" This will solve the problem. If all the brothers and sisters with such a problem would go to the Lord to submit themselves to the Lord and take the headship of Christ, the problem is solved.

REALIZING THE HEADSHIP OF CHRIST
IN A PRACTICAL WAY

The order in the church comes from the headship of Christ being realized by us in a practical way. If each of us submits ourself to the headship of Christ and takes His lordship in a real way, there will be no problem. There will be no argument; rather, a nice, spiritual order will spontaneously come into being among us. We will get nowhere by doctrines, teachings, and arguments. We can argue everyday until the Lord comes back, but we will not solve the problems. However, if each one of us would submit to the headship of Christ and pray, "Lord, You are the Head, and I realize Your headship in my life in a practical way," every problem will be solved. Problems are solved not by doctrine or by teaching but by realizing the headship of Christ.

I must speak seriously. Do you realize that there is a rebellious nature within us? There is an element, an essence, within us that is always rebelling. The problem in the church is one of rebellion; no one likes to submit to others. This damages and spoils the church life. I beg you to take this word from one of your brothers. If we are going to practice the church life with sincerity, we must submit ourselves to the headship of Christ and realize the headship of the Lord. Otherwise, there is no way for us to practice the real church life. We can come together all the time, but we will not have the reality of the church life. We will only be false, just pretending and presuming; we will not be real. To have the real church life, we need to submit. We should not try to submit to others; we should simply submit to the headship of Christ. Then we will be right in the order in the church. This is not an issue between us and others; it is an issue between us and the Head. If there is a problem between brothers or sisters, that means there is a problem between us and Christ the Head. To be sure, if we are right with the Head, we will be right with others. It is possible for us to realize the real church life only when we realize the headship of the Lord in a practical way.

We are not going to organize something among the Christians, and we have no intention to set up a church of another kind. No, that is something fallen; that is not the Lord's recovery. Rather, we are very burdened that in these last days the Lord will recover a real church life among His children to express Christ and to bring the coming kingdom of God. There is a great need of the real church life. The real church life requires that we know how to exercise ourselves to apply Christ as our life and realize His headship among us. We live by Him, and we live under Him. He is our life, and He is our

Head. This is the only way for us to practice the real church life, and this is the only way for all the problems to be solved.

None of the problems are solved by discussion or argument. The history of the church proves that arguments never get us anywhere. In fact, the more we argue, the more trouble and problems we have. Let us submit ourselves to the headship of Christ. We need to practice to take the Lord as the Head and to realize His headship among us in a practical way. If we are going to argue with a brother, we must first check with ourself and ask, "Am I under the headship of Christ?" If we check in this way, our argument will be gone. The headship of the Lord is the answer to our arguments.

Let us see clearly that in the church there is the need of a spiritual order, and this order comes only from the headship of Christ being realized by us in a practical way. Without this, there is no possibility for us to practice the real church life. We look to the Lord for this matter. This is very basic and very vital. If we have this, we have the church life. If we do not have this, the church life is gone.

CHAPTER FOUR

THE CHARTER OF THE CHURCH

In this chapter we will consider the charter of the church. Although there is not such a word as *charter* in the New Testament, there may not be another word to express this aspect of the church. *Charter* refers to the rules, regulations, and bylaws of the church. Today every Christian organization of a certain size has its rules, regulations, and bylaws, but we must come back to the Scriptures to see the charter ordained by God. If we read the New Testament carefully, repeatedly, and purposefully, we will see that it is hard to find rules, regulations, and bylaws for the church. Strictly speaking, there are no such items in the New Testament. From the account of the formation of the church on the day of Pentecost in Acts 2 to the end of the New Testament, there are not any rules, regulations, and bylaws for the church. In the first few chapters of Acts, we cannot find such matters in the church in Jerusalem. Peter, John, and the other early apostles did not lay down any rules in order to form the church.

We must speak of the charter of the church because many saints have the thought that if we are going to practice the church life, we must have certain rules, regulations, and bylaws. Some have said that we do not have written bylaws, but we have understood ones. However, not only should we have no written rules, but we should also have no understood rules. In fact, we should have no kind of outward rules, regulations, and bylaws for the church. Rather, we should have a spiritual charter of the church, the spiritual rules and regulations for the church.

THE CROSS

The first spiritual regulation of the church is the cross. The church comes into being by Christ, but the cross of Christ is the very means through which and by which Christ brings the church into being. The New Testament speaks mainly of Christ, the cross, the church, and the kingdom. Christ accomplished His work on the cross, Christ brought the church into being through the cross, and the church brings in the kingdom. Without Christ there is no cross, without the cross the church cannot be brought into being, and without the church there is no possibility for the kingdom to come. Therefore, Christ is first, the cross is second, the church is third, and the kingdom is fourth. Without Christ there is no source of the church, and without the cross there is no means for the church to be brought into being. Therefore, the cross is the rule and regulation of the church.

Now we must consider how Christ brought the church into being through the cross. Christ brought all negative things, including sin, sins, the soul, the flesh, the self, Satan, the evil world, and death, to the cross. The cross has dealt with and put away all these negative things. Sin, sins, the self, the flesh, world, and Satan cannot pass through the cross. Therefore, the church does not come before the cross; it comes after the cross. The cross is a test and a checkpoint, and after crossing the checkpoint we come to the church.

When foreigners come into this country, they must first pass a checkpoint so that everything they have can be examined. Before I entered this country for the third time, some friends in the Philippines gave me some mangos to enjoy and share with others in this country. However, the checkpoint at the airport did not allow me to bring in these wonderful items. They told me that I could not pass through with them. We have to follow the regulations at the checkpoint, or we will not be allowed to enter the country. Similarly, outside the door of the church there is a checkpoint, which is the cross. When we come to the church, we have to put our "mangos" on the cross and leave them there. This means that we must put our sins, our self, our flesh, the worldly things, Satan, and all things of death on the cross. The cross must check us, and we must pass through this checkpoint in order to come to the church.

Have you been checked at the cross? Before coming to the church, have you been regulated by the cross? I can never forget a message given by Brother Watchman Nee in which he said that at the entrance of the church there is the cross. When we come to the church, we must pass through the cross. If we come into the church without being checked at the cross, we will be a danger to the church. This means that we have not been regulated, that there is no rule with us, and we are coming to the church in a wild and natural way, a way that is not ruled and regulated. The rule and regulation is the cross. The cross must check, regulate, and rule us.

We do not have an outward charter, but we do have a spiritual charter, the first item of which is the cross. To pass the cross is the first regulation, the first item of the spiritual charter of the church. When a brother comes to the elders' meeting to suggest something or to raise a point, he must first pass through the first item of the spiritual charter of the church, that is, the cross. He must pass the cross and be checked by the cross. He must check, "Is my flesh, my self, my personal desire, my will, my mind, my idea, and my thought on the cross?" If one is not checked by the cross and comes to the elders' meeting in a natural way, he will be a damage to the elders' meeting and to the entire church.

From my past experience I can testify that nearly every time the responsible brothers of the church have come together, we first have knelt down to pray, "Lord, before we discuss anything about the church, check us with the cross." Then when a brother brings something to the meeting, the cross checks him and he asks, "Is this something worldly? Can it pass the cross?" If he checks in this way, he will immediately be clear. He may say, "Lord, this is something worldly. Forgive me. I must put it on the cross." I can never forget how in a certain elders' meeting a problem was raised, and a brother began to quarrel. After speaking two sentences, he said, "Brothers, I will stop here. Please forgive me because I spoke in my self and in the flesh." This is the regulation of the cross. If we want to practice the real church life, we must pass through the cross and be checked by the cross. The cross is the very means by which the Lord has dealt with all negative things. We cannot pass through the cross with anything negative.

From my past experiences I can tell you that it is not simple to practice the church life with the saints. In the church life there is every kind of person. We cannot say why there are so many peculiar people among us Christians. What can we do? A number of times I was forced to tell someone, "In what you are speaking, have you passed through the cross?" This is the best way to stop people from speaking in a fleshly way. If we ask the brothers in this way, they will realize in their conscience that they have not passed through the cross.

However, we must be careful when we ask people this. In order to check with people in this way, we must first check whether we ourselves have passed through the cross. In my hometown in North China around 1937, the responsible brothers were still young. Once in the meeting of the responsible brothers a brother spoke something from his flesh. I asked him, "Do you think that you are in the spirit and that you have passed through the cross to say this?" He replied, "Brother Lee, do you think that you are in the spirit and have passed through the cross to check with me?" After this, I did not say anything, and my tears nearly dropped. The next morning, that brother came to me with tears, saying that he had been unable to sleep for the entire night. He said that he had been in the flesh, and he asked me to forgive him. In the next meeting of the responsible brothers, he was the first one to speak. He asked all the brothers to forgive him for what he had done, and we consoled him. To be sure, by this we can see what the regulation in the church is. The first item of regulation is the cross.

CHRIST AS LIFE

The second item of the spiritual charter of the church is Christ as life. On the negative side, the cross deals with all the negative opinions, thoughts, differing concepts, ideas, and desires and the things of the self, of the world, and of sin. On the positive side, the cross released Christ as life. The death of the Lord was His release. The more we pass through the cross, the more Christ is released. If we would learn the lessons of the cross, Christ the Lord will be much more released among us. This is something not negative but positive. We do not have regulations in letters, but we have the regulations in life, which is Christ. For us all to take Christ as life and to take nothing else is a wonderful rule, regulation, and bylaw for the church. By the sovereignty of the Lord, we have experienced this wonderful rule in recent years. Nearly every time that we have come together to serve the Lord, we have experienced Christ.

We must be careful to check whether or not we are according to this regulation of the spiritual charter of the church. We check ourselves by asking, "Is this something of Christ as life?" This is not a doctrinal matter but one that we must put into practice. When we, as the brothers and sisters who come together to practice the church life, discuss or suggest something, we must check and ask, "Lord, is this something of You? Is this something of life?" If it is not of life, we drop it. We do not insist on such things; we simply drop them. We must check ourselves by Christ as life. If we do this, we will save ourselves much trouble. We will not have troubles if we check ourselves by Christ as life.

After we pass through the cross, Christ is released as the reality of the church. If we do not have Christ as life, we do not have the church life. The church life is simply Christ realized by us in a corporate way. We are not a religious organization. We are a group of persons who are saved, regenerated, and indwelt by the Holy Spirit, coming together to experience Christ in a corporate way. What we suggest must be Christ Himself as life to us. If we keep this regulation, how wonderful the church will be!

This is not merely a doctrine. Recently, some friends have come to me and asked, "Brother Lee, what kind of regulations and rules do you have?" This is hard to answer. I would not say that we have regulations, and neither would I say that we do not have regulations. To be sure, we have regulations, but they are not the regulations in letters. They are the regulations in Christ Himself. The first regulation of the church is the cross, and the second is Christ as life. If we would take this word and check ourselves, others, and the entire church by these regulations, we will see how wonderful the church life will be. This will save us from many things.

THE HOLY SPIRIT

The third item of the spiritual charter of the church is the Holy Spirit in our spirit. The Spirit of God, the Spirit of Christ, the Spirit of life, is the living regulation. Therefore, there is no need for us to have regulations in letters. A history of the creeds of the church, containing all the different creeds since the apostolic fathers, requires several large volumes. In the past years many people have asked me what kind of creed we have. I always like to tell people that we do not have a creed; rather, we have the cross, we have Christ, and we have the Spirit of God. These are the items of the spiritual charter of the church. When we come to practice the church life, we need the Holy Spirit as our living creed.

We may claim to know the Holy Spirit as our creed more than we know the cross. However, without the cross, we may even misuse and abuse the teaching concerning the Spirit. One aspect of the Holy Spirit in this age, or dispensation, of grace is illustrated in the holy Scriptures by the rain from heaven. Many people receive the rain, but they misuse and abuse what they receive. If we check ourselves with the cross, and we honor, magnify, exalt, and respect the Lord Jesus Christ, we are in the right position to properly experience the Holy Spirit. We must be checked by the cross, and we must be safeguarded by Christ. Then we will experience the Spirit in a proper and adequate way.

The Spirit is our charter. Whenever we come together, we must do everything in the Spirit. When we come to discuss something, we must discuss it in the Spirit. If we do not have the anointing Spirit within us, we should stop, be silent, and give up our idea. If there is no registration, confirmation, or seal from the Holy Spirit, we need to stop. In recent years, by the mercy and grace of the Lord, I have learned the lesson never to argue or quarrel with people. Many times people argue with me, but I ask them, "Do you have the inner anointing at this very moment while you are speaking?" This checks where we are. If we check whether or not we have the anointing, we will know what to do. If we do not have the anointing, we will stop.

There are no outward regulations among us; our regulation is the cross, Christ, and the Spirit. If we do not have the Spirit, we have nothing to do or to say; we are through. We may be right in everything, but we may be short of one thing; we may be short of the Holy Spirit with the anointing.

THE HEADSHIP OF CHRIST

The fourth item of the spiritual charter of the church is the headship of Christ. We do not have outward regulations, but we have the regulating Head. We have the Lord Christ as the Head to always regulate us. We are under His headship, submitting to His authority. We need to check ourselves with the cross, Christ, the Holy Spirit, and the headship. Are we under the Head of the church? The headship alone of the Lord Christ will regulate us and rule out many problems and mistakes.

Day by day all the members of our physical body are regulated by our head. All the members cannot do as they like or act as they desire. A hand may want to strike a brother, but the head regulates it and makes it stop. If we mean business to say that we are of Christ, we must realize that the Lord Christ is our Head. We not only love Him, but we respect Him as the Head, and we are under the headship, the authority, of the Head. This is our regulation. If we do not know the headship of the Lord Jesus, and if we cannot bring the believers to realize the headship, there is no possibility among us of practicing the church life. When we come together, instead of having Christ as our one Head, we will be like a man with many heads. When we lose the Head, every member becomes a head, but if we simply take Christ as the Head, every member is submissive, and all are regulated by the headship of Christ. Whatever we do, practice, and suggest in the church must be checked as to whether it is under the headship of Christ. This is the regulation of being checked by the cross, by Christ, by the Spirit, and by the headship of Christ.

THE BODY

The fifth item of the spiritual charter of the church is the Body of Christ. We must be regulated, restricted, and limited by the Body. In 1939 Brother Watchman Nee went to Europe and was absent from China for a year and a half. During this time, the brothers and sisters who were seeking and serving the Lord realized from their experience that when the bread and cup are being passed in the Lord's table meeting, it is better for everyone to contact and enjoy the Lord in the spirit in a quiet way. At that time, we were able to sense the Lord's presence very much during the passing of the bread and the cup. However, since Brother Nee was absent during this time, he was not aware of this new practice. When he returned, he attended a Lord's table meeting. When the cup was blessed and passed to the brothers, he received the anointing and inspiration to sing a hymn, but one of the elders told him that it was better to be silent. Brother Nee was happy to be stopped. I was sitting very close to him, and I saw everything that happened. I believe that Brother Nee had the inspiration. He was not a careless or childish man but rather was full of spiritual experience. However, he was under the regulation of the Body and went along with the Body. We must learn how to be restricted and limited by the Body.

Watchman Nee's mother was a dear and lovely sister, who had a number of spiritual gifts. She was active, positive, living, and she wrote a book as a testimony to the Lord. In 1948 we had some conference meetings with several hundred people, and for the first few days she would offer a living prayer every night. However, we felt that her prayer did not fit the need in those meetings. We may illustrate this with clothing. If someone needs a tie, we should not offer him a belt. Even a valuable belt does not fit the need for a tie. Sister Nee's prayer was nice, living, bold, and strong, but all the leading ones felt that it did not fit the need. However, since she was elderly and beloved, we did not know what to do. After the meetings a few of the leading ones would fellowship about the conference. On the third night of meeting in this way, Brother Nee told me to take a pencil and paper to write a short letter to our elderly sister, saying, "Sister Nee, after we heard your prayers in the meetings in the last few days, we all feel that they do not fit. We remind you to be limited, and we ask that from now on you do not pray such prayers in the meetings. The Lord be with you." Brother Nee, I, and an elderly co-working sister signed the letter, and we gave it to Sister Nee. The next day before the start of the meeting, she came to me in tears and said, "Brother Lee, praise the Lord!" Although her feeling was deep, this word from her indicated that she took the fellowship. The limitation and restriction of the Body is lovely.

If we would realize the limitation of the Body in this way, the Lord will be with us very much. We should always consider whether we are justified by the Body in whatever we do. We must question, "In acting in this way, am I justified by the Body? Will all the brothers and sisters be happy if I do this? When I behave in the meetings in such a way, are the brothers happy with me?" We must check ourselves by the brothers, by the Body. Sometimes I even say to the brothers, "Tell me frankly; tell me the truth. Do you feel happy with what I am doing? I am waiting to express your feeling." This is the pleasant restriction of the Body.

BEING GENERAL

The sixth item of the spiritual charter of the church is to be general. When we come to others, we do not have anything special to insist upon. We are open and general. We simply come together to fellowship, discuss, pray, and seek the Lord's hand. Then we all agree with how the Lord leads us, and we advance by one step. Otherwise, we wait. If we are going to realize the real church life, we must be general.

By *general,* we mean that we have the Lord Jesus as our Savior, our Lord, our life, and everything to us. Moreover, we do not agree with anything that damages the church. These are the things on which we insist, but besides these, we are completely general. Someone may believe in baptism by immersion, and he may practice it, but he must not insist upon it. It may be that a certain percentage of the Lord's children do not agree with this practice. If we insist on it, we will have different opinions.

We may keep a certain practice because we feel it is right, but when we come to the church we must be general. If we are not general, we have something as a specialty; then we will create trouble and be sectarian. If some brothers and sisters insist upon baptism by immersion, and others insist on baptism by sprinkling, they will fight. Where then will the church life be? The church life will be gone. We must not insist on these things and fight with the Lord's children. We may believe that baptism by sprinkling is sufficient, but we do not insist on it. Rather, we come to one another in a very general way with a very general attitude. Then others can take the same attitude, and we can kneel down before the Lord and pray, "Lord, what do You lead us to do?" This is the right way to practice the church life.

Some dear and strong saints who are very much for the Lord simply do not agree with speaking in tongues. They oppose it and say that it is wrong and even devilish. This kind of attitude is not right. It is too extreme. We should not oppose speaking in tongues, but in the same principle, if we speak in tongues in a genuine way, we should simply praise the Lord for His mercy. We may keep this practice, but we should not bring it to the church to push it and insist upon it. Many dear, lovely brothers and sisters may not feel happy if someone speaks in tongues in the meeting, so that person must be general. Someone may speak in tongues but still come to the meeting in a general way, having nothing as a specialty. Let us not make a regulation as to whether or not we should speak in tongues in the meeting. Let us open to the Lord, be general with one another, and leave this matter to the Lord. If some saints do not agree with speaking in tongues, for their sake we drop it for the time being. Likewise, we deal with all things in this way.

The one thing we must insist upon is that the Lord Jesus is everything to us. We cannot give this up. If someone speaks to oppose the Lord Jesus, we must stand and fight their speaking, but with all other things we must be general. We must be special in nothing. We may have something else, but we are not special in it. If we are special in anything, we are sectarian. We may come together with many different backgrounds and experiences, but when we come together, we come in a general way with a general attitude. We do not insist on anything. If someone likes something and feels good about it, as long as it is not something against the Lord Himself, we are willing to go along with him in a general way.

However, it is not easy to be general. Even if we go to the Lord to be checked by Him, there may still be something in us that we insist upon. If we insist on opposing speaking in tongues, we are wrong, and if we insist on speaking in tongues, we are also wrong. We must be very open, general, and objective with one another. We do not take the way of the denominations, such as the Mennonites, the Brethren, the Methodists, or any other kind. We are general, open, and objective before the Lord. We come together as the local saints of the Lord to practice the Body life without any outward regulations. Moreover, we drop our own backgrounds. In all my time in this country, I have not insisted on anything from the churches in the Far East. We should not bring in our own backgrounds.

Let us be completely general, open, and objective in our coming together. Let us come together and pray and fellowship. We all, and especially the leading ones, need more time to pray together. We should not do things according to our past experience, and we should not make decisions according to our background or past knowledge. The leading ones should pray much in a living, new, and fresh way and even fast before the Lord. Then we can let the Lord lead us on in a new way, a way not according to other things, but according to the living, present, fresh, and new guidance of the Holy Spirit in each moment and in each matter. This is the right way. I am very concerned about the meeting of the leading brothers. We do not come together to pray enough. We should forget about the past, all the problems in the church, and the church affairs, and spend more time to pray, even to fast, and to seek the Lord, asking, "Lord, what is Your mind? What is your purpose and guiding today for our going on?" This is a living way, but this requires each one of us to drop and forget our past.

We must not bring our past experience, background, doctrine, teaching, and influences into the church. If we do this, we are sectarian. We must be very general. We must not feel that we like something or do not like something. If we like something, it may be that the Lord does not like it, or if we do not like something, perhaps the Lord does like it. Let us open completely to the Lord and to one another, and let us be completely general. Are we willing to do this? It is not easy.

A brother from the West who went to the East came to me one day, saying, "We Christians in the West always seat the brothers and the sisters together. Why do you here seat sisters on one side and brothers on the other side? I simply cannot go along with this." It seems that this brother could only be happy with his own way. We should not bring our background to the church. We should come to the church not with anything of our past but simply with an open spirit and a general heart, completely open to the Lord, to the church, and to the children of the Lord in order to fellowship, wait, pray, and seek the Lord. The living Lord will bring us the living guidance for the present moment. This is the right way.

We must not complain about others or make claims upon others; we must simply check ourselves. Do we come to practice the church with something in our heart upon which we insist? We should not say, "We agree with this, but we will not agree with that." Rather, we must be very open and general, not insisting on or pushing anything of our past or background. We love the Lord and respect Him, and we love His church, His Body, and His saints. Let us come together without insisting on anything. We are open and general, we pray and have living fellowship with the Lord and with one another, and we let the Lord lead us in a new and fresh way. If we do this, the Lord will go a long way among us, and many wonderful things will come out because we have paved a free way for the Lord. The Lord will be freed; He will not be bound by us.

THE WORD OF GOD

The seventh and last item of the spiritual charter of the church is the Word of God. Concerning so many important, vital matters we must be checked by the Word. It is not necessary to say much at this time, because many of us already realize this.

The spiritual charter of the church is the cross, Christ, the Holy Spirit, the headship of Christ, the Body, a general attitude, and the Word of God. If we are going to practice the real church life, we must take all these matters and put them into practice. If we keep these seven items of the spiritual charter of the church, the church will be helped by us. If we are checked by these few items, we will become a positive help to the church. Otherwise, we will be a damage, a hindrance, and even a danger to the church life. May the Lord be merciful to us.

CHAPTER FIVE

THE PRAYER OF THE CHURCH

Scripture Reading: Acts 2:42; 4:23-24, 29-31; 12:5, 12

In this chapter we shall see something concerning the prayer life in the practice of the church life. Strictly speaking, there is no outward charter in the church. Rather, what the church should have is a prayer life. There is a great difference between the way people practice Christian churches today and the record of the churches in the book of Acts. Today people practice to have rules, regulations, creeds, and an outward charter, but in Acts we cannot find such things. The churches did not have outward regulations and rules. What they had was a church life in prayer.

Prayer was the initiation of the church's existence. The first local church, the first expression of the church, came into being through the prayer of the one hundred twenty for ten days. They did not have written regulations or a charter for an organization. What they had was ten days of prayer. They prayed and prayed until one day something happened, not of themselves, but from God. That was the formation of the first local church. That was the way that the first expression of the Lord's Body came into being.

CONTINUING STEADFASTLY IN THE TEACHING AND THE FELLOWSHIP OF THE APOSTLES, IN THE BREAKING OF BREAD AND THE PRAYERS

After its formation, the early church continued in four things (Acts 2:42). The first is the teaching of the apostles. To keep the teaching of the apostles is to keep the teaching of the Lord, because the teaching of the apostles is the teaching of the Lord. The disciples had to be taught so that they could be transformed in many ways. If we read the first few chapters of Acts, we will see that in the early days, when the church was first formed, all the members of the first expression of the Lord's Body were brought to the point that they gave up their concepts, their background, and their makeup from the past in order to receive something new. They did this by receiving and keeping the word of the Lord, which was passed on to them through the apostles. There is no hint or trace that they held on to anything from their past. In their living and even in their inner way of life, by the power of the Holy Spirit they gave up their way and everything of the past, and they came to the word of the Lord to receive something new. This is the correct meaning of continuing steadfastly in the teaching of the apostles.

In this way, the disciples were not only saved and forgiven by the Lord; they were truly regenerated, and their regeneration included a certain measure of transformation. They were at least transformed in their way of human life. In their way of conducting themselves, they forgot all that they had in the past and gave up their background. They came to the word, the Lord's teachings, to take everything in a new way. At that time, they did not take the Lord's word in the way of theory; rather, they learned the Lord's word in a practical way. They did not study theology, but they learned how to follow the Lord, how to have a daily life in a new way, and how to have a church life. They were regenerated and transformed to the extent that they gave up everything in the past and took a new way to live, to work, to serve the Lord, and to have the church life.

The second matter in which the disciples continued is the fellowship of the apostles. Fellowship is a communion in the life of the Lord and in the Spirit of the Lord. By this fellowship they became practically one in the Spirit and in life. The word *fellowship* is a special word, which in Greek includes the meaning of bringing into oneness. Such a oneness can only be in the Spirit, by the Spirit, and in the divine life. The disciples all learned how to give up their old way of human living and even their own life to live by the divine life, the life of the Lord, and to walk in the Holy Spirit. They were taught how to

live by the Lord as their life and how to walk in the Holy
Spirit. In this Spirit they were brought into oneness practically; this is the real fellowship.

When we read the first four or five chapters of Acts, we
can see that the disciples were truly one, not only in the inner
life but also in their outward living. They had the fellowship
in life practically. This is different from the practice of many
of today's Christians. When many Christians come together
to have a meeting, they greet one another nicely and then say
goodbye. They are nice to each other, but they do not know
each other's real situation and condition. This is not the real
fellowship. The real fellowship is the oneness in the Spirit
and in the divine life. The disciples even held their material
possessions in common. They gave up their own way of life,
and they gave up their own life itself. They took the Lord
Jesus as their life, and they took the Holy Spirit for their
living. In this way, they were brought to such a point that
they could be one practically in their daily living. This is the
true meaning of fellowship. Fellowship is not merely to shake
hands and greet one another. It is to be brought into oneness
in the Spirit, in the divine life, and in the spiritual living.

The third matter in which the disciples continued was the
breaking of bread. This was not only to remember the Lord
but to exhibit Him, testify of Him, and to testify of the life
they had. The Lord's table is not only a remembrance but also
a testimony. We who have been saved and regenerated by
the Lord and who are continually living by the Lord come
together as an exhibition to show to the entire universe—
especially to the principalities, powers, dominions, and
authorities in the heavenlies—what kind of life we have and
how we are living. We live by Jesus as our life, and the life we
have is simply the Lord Christ Himself. He is our life. He is
the living bread, and we enjoy Him day by day. Then we come
together to remember Him and testify to the whole universe.

The fourth and last item of the early church life is the life
of prayer. The disciples had no weapons, no charter, and no
worldly wisdom or power. What they had was a living God,
and they brought all things to this living God; they brought
all their problems to this living Lord. This is the real meaning

of their prayer. The church life in the early days was a life of prayer. If we compare this to today's Christianity, we will see a difference. In today's Christianity there are many teachings, human ways, organizations, charters, regulations, rules, material things, and other matters, but there is very little prayer. If we are going to practice the real church life, we must learn how to pray in a practical, prevailing, living, and fresh way. Moreover, we must learn how to help others to pray and make every member of the church a praying member.

Many times someone asks me how a member of the church can be a functioning member. If we expect a member of the church to be a functioning member, we must help him or her to learn how to pray. There is no other way. A praying member is a functioning member, but if a member does not have a prayer life, he can never be a functioning member. We must learn to pray, and we must learn how to help others to pray.

If we are going to have a real church life, we must learn how to have a prayer life and even pray with fasting. What I feel most deeply in these days is the lack of prayer in the church. I would almost rather give up the time for speaking these messages and use all our time for prayer. We must learn to pray, and we must learn how to pray in a corporate way, as the church coming together, as a part of the church life. This is a vital, much needed matter today.

THE NEED FOR THE LEADING ONES
AND SERVING ONES TO PRAY

The service of a leading one, an elder, a deacon, or a serving one in the church, is firstly a matter of prayer. We must pray concerning the responsibility of the church. All the leading ones must come together to pray. It is hard enough to pray by ourselves, but to ask all the leading ones and serving ones to come together to pray is more difficult. The biggest reason for this is that we do not have the oneness. When the leading ones come together, one comes with his mind, another comes with his thought, another comes with his concept, and everyone else comes with his own idea. Everyone comes trying to convince others, having the intention, desire, and hope to push something each feels is important. This kills the church life, it kills the meeting of the leading ones, and it kills the leading ones' way to bear responsibility. Then as long as the leading ones' way to bear responsibility is killed, the entire church life is gone. Therefore, we must learn never to bring something to impose on others. We must always try not to convince others but simply to have the oneness and pray together. Brothers, let us forget our opinion and thought and come together to pray. Let the Lord break through, come in, and speak to us.

I am not speaking something that I do not know. In the past many years I have had many experiences, and I can testify that where there is a group of leading ones who know how to pray in this way, there the church is very strong, prevailing, and living. On the contrary, where there is a group of leading ones who know nothing of this kind of prayer, but who only know to argue a cause, to debate, to fight, and to convince one another, there the church is a dead church. It is shameful that in many dead churches many of the leading ones are very zealous. They are very much for doctrines and teachings, but they are too much for doctrines and teachings. Each one thinks that he is right, knowing more than others. A brother may seem to know something about spiritual matters, but he always insists on what he knows. When he comes together with the leading ones, he always knows the way to convince them all. However, he may not know how to go into the presence of the Lord and how to go to the Lord with others to contact the Lord and let the Lord have the opportunity to speak and reveal something. I am simply speaking what I have seen in the past. This is the biggest problem in the church today.

I advise and even beg those who are the leading brothers of the church first to practice to forget about all the things of the past and come together to pray. If we say that we are going to practice the church life, we should pray about it rather than discuss it. If we open the door to merely discuss the church life, we open the door to let the enemy come in and bring in many opinions and thoughts. The best way to shut the door and shut out all the opinions is to pray. Let us kneel down, not to speak our thoughts or opinions, but to pray and let the Lord speak. However, it may be that very few leading ones do this. Whenever we come together there is always the temptation to discuss. First one brother opens his mouth to speak a small word to express a thought, and then the second, third, fourth, and fifth brothers follow to do the same. Then all the time is gone. Moreover, the more they discuss, the more they are not of one mind. To discuss simply opens the door to the enemy.

PRAYER BEING THE ONLY WAY
TO PRACTICE THE CHURCH LIFE

If we are going to learn to pray with others in such a way, we must first give up our self and our own thoughts. We honor the Lord, we respect the Lord, and we implore the Lord, "Lord, we come to You to seek Your mind. We bring ourselves into Your presence to give You the full opportunity to speak something." We need to pray in such a way. I hate any other way to practice the church. Some people today say, "We are practicing the New Testament church," and some even seek to practice the church life outwardly according to *The Normal Christian Church Life*. This is wrong. The only right way to practice the church life is to go to the Lord to pray.

We are not following an outward way, and we will not copy a certain way. This is something dead. We must go to the Lord and pray to open a new way for Him to come in. We must pray for the present situation concerning what the Lord will speak and what He will do. We must pray each day until we all see the same thing and have the same inner anointing and the same assurance. If we do not have the anointing and the assurance, we need to pray again even with fasting and without sleep. This is the only way to practice the church life.

It is even wrong to say that we are going to practice the church life according to the book of Acts. We should not say, "Here is something in Acts which the apostles practiced in the early days. Let us do the same thing today." This is merely to copy the apostles in the way of dead letters. This has no life, no anointing, and no impact. Rather, we must pray. We must bring our present situation, our need, and all things in prayer to the Lord and pray continually until all the leading ones have the same anointing and the same assurance that they see something of the Lord for us today. Then there will be the freshness, the newness, the anointing, and the impact. The Lord will honor this.

It is easy to speak about this, but to practice this kind of prayer is very difficult. If we try to pray in this way, we will discover where we are. If we come together merely to discuss something, everyone will be very active, but if we try to kneel down to pray, after a few minutes some may begin to sleep. They simply have no interest in this kind of prayer. Instead, they want to know what they should do. One of the largest cities in China, with a population of more than one million, was a big field for the Lord's work with much potential. However, the church there did not have any improvement for a number of years, and the news of their troubles and problems always came to us. One day we were led by the Lord to go there to pray with them for a certain period of time. Then I discovered that they did not have many problems; they had only one, the problem of quarreling. Whenever they came together, they only knew to quarrel with one another. They even quarreled in front of us concerning the hospitality that they were to render us.

After I discovered this problem, I suggested that the leading ones and serving ones come together to pray. They all agreed to come, but to my impression they all came ready to argue. I did my best to stop the arguing. I said, "Brothers and sisters, let us kneel down and pray." However, when we knelt down, no one began to pray. I was forced to start the prayer, but after I prayed, no one continued. Then I prayed a second time, but still no one continued. When we rose up, everyone smiled pleasantly and prepared to listen to what I was going to say. This condition killed the church. I stayed with them for many weeks until they were somewhat helped to realize what their problem was.

I wish to recommend to you that the best, proper, and only way to practice the church is to pray in a new way. It is not to pray in an old way to convince others or to ask the Lord to help us to convince others. We must give up every idea or thought to pray in this way. Forget this way and come to the Lord in a new way to pray, to let the Lord come in, and to let Him speak something. If we do not learn how to pray corporately in a new way, the church can never be prevailing.

On the one hand, before we come to practice the church life, we first must read the Scriptures and many spiritual teachings. We should know how the Methodists, Presbyterians, Baptists, Anglicans, Lutherans, and others practice the church. We should also know the way practiced in the Epistles and taught in *The Normal Christian Church Life* and other proper writings. On the other hand, however, in order to practice the church life in a living and prevailing way, we must not depend on all those teachings. Lay them all aside and simply go to the Lord to pray in a living and new way. This is the right way. To follow others by copying them does not work. There is no life, impact, or freshness in that. We need the freshness, newness, impact, life, anointing, power, and authority, and there is no other way to have this but by prayer.

Moreover, we must pray sufficiently, pray through, and pray in a new way. We should not have a formula in our mind and bring it to the Lord to ask Him to perform it. This is the wrong way to pray. Many times people have a formula which they bring to the Lord and ask Him to carry it out according to their own way. This does not work. We must come to the Lord like a sheet of blank, white paper, saying, "Lord, here we are. Write on us. Impress us with what Your mind is and what You want to do." This requires strength, energy, patience, and travailing in the spirit. There is no quicker way. The practice of the church is not a quick matter. We must pay a price for it in the spirit.

PRAYING TO FIGHT THE SPIRITUAL WARFARE

Whenever there is a problem or a need, we may declare a fast among the whole church, whether for one meal or for a whole day. The whole church must go to the Lord and pray. There is no other way to solve the problems, to have the Lord's guidance, and to bring the Lord's people into spiritual reality. I can testify regarding this. For many years even up until this day, the elders in the church in Taipei have come together a number of times each week. Only one such time is to take care of the saints' affairs; all the rest are simply to pray, mostly early in the morning. When they come together, they do not discuss anything. They simply start to pray. They do this several times a week for every week of the year.

The aspect of the church that the enemy, Satan, fears the most is the prayer of the church. Brother Andrew Murray said that whenever the church kneels down to pray, Satan trembles. Satan trembles at the church's prayer. The practice of the church is not merely a temporary, human matter on the earth. The practice of the church is spiritual, and it affects the spiritual world very much. It involves a real warfare. The Lord told us clearly that He would build His church and that the gates of Hades would not prevail against it. This indicates that whenever and wherever there is the building up of the church, there is the activity of the gates of Hades against it. We know this, and we have experienced this. Therefore, there is the need of a fighting prayer; there is the need for some to pray to fight the spiritual battle.

PRACTICAL DETAILS CONCERNING PRAYER

Here we may point out some practical details concerning the prayer of the church. In order to have a prayer life, especially a corporate prayer life, the prayer life of the church, we must learn to consecrate ourselves. If we have never consecrated ourselves to the Lord, it is impossible to have a real church life. If we are going to have prayer as our life, we must first go to the Lord, telling Him, "Lord, here I am. I consecrate and offer to You my whole being, my whole person, without any kind of reservation." We must have the definite consecration of our whole being, and every time we pray, we must take this basic standing, saying, "Lord, we come to pray on the ground of consecration."

Second, we must confess our sins. We must deal with our sins and our conscience, making our conscience void of offense, pure, good, and right. In dealing in this way, we must apply the Lord's blood. In my own experience, whenever I go to the Lord, I spend much time to clear my conscience so that

I can pray. I sense the need of the cleansing and covering of the Lord's blood. Even when I come to pray with the brothers, I pray, "Lord, cleanse us with Your precious blood." In many places, however, the brothers I pray with fail to practice this. Sometimes I question, "Am I the most sinful one?" First John 1:5-9 says that God is light, and that if we have fellowship with Him, we walk in the light, and the issue of our being in the light is that we sense the need of the application of the cleansing of the blood of the Son of God. To be sure, when we are in the light, that is, in the presence of God, we will say, "Lord, forgive me and cleanse me with Your precious blood." We need to confess, deal with sins, and deal with our conscience.

Third, after we take the ground of consecration, and after we confess all our sins and deal with our conscience, we have peace, clarity, and transparency in our conscience. Then we must thoroughly learn the lesson to pray not according to what we know, what we remember, what we desire, or what we think but simply to pray according to the inner anointing. This is essential for individual prayer as well as for corporate prayer. Moreover, we should not care about our sentences or grammar. We may simply pray in broken sentences and broken language.

Fourth, we should never try to correct or convince others in prayer. Rather, we should be transparent and transcendent. We should not touch earthly differences, but be transcendent. In our prayer we should not "take a car" to drive among the situations; we should rather "take the airplane" and fly above them. We should never try to convert, convince, or correct others in prayer. This is not real prayer, and it does not work.

MAKING THE CHURCH IN OUR LOCALITY
A PRAYING CHURCH

We should learn these practical matters and practice them in our prayer, especially in the corporate prayer. We need to consecrate, confess, and pray according to the inner anointing. We should never try to touch others through our prayer but simply let the Lord touch them directly. Then something new will come out. The leading ones especially must pray much, even more than others, and they must help others to have a real prayer life. They should help all the brothers to pray, one by one. The problem today is that when we have a message meeting, many people come, but when there is a prayer meeting, only one-third of the saints come. It is as if some say, "If there is a message, I will come, but if it is only prayer, I will stay home and rest." In some denominations, it is possible that only three people come to the prayer meeting: the pastor, his wife, and the custodian. Then when they sing a hymn, the pastor plays the piano, the wife leads the singing, and the custodian follows. I have seen such a situation. In some places, only two of the five leading ones come to the prayer meeting, while the other three stay away. With only a few in the prayer meeting, that church is the weakest one. The normal condition, however, is that there are more in the prayer meeting than in the other meetings. If when the church has a prayer meeting, all the believers come, that church will be the most prevailing. It will be a living church. We should pray by ourselves and help others to pray. We must make the church in our locality a praying church. Take this word and try to practice it. Then we will see the difficulties, on the one hand, but on the other hand, we will see the blessing.

To start this kind of prayer is not easy for several reasons. One is that the enemy would never willinglys allow the church to practice this kind of prayer. Therefore, we must be patient to fight the battle. To be sure, we must pray. If we cannot get through, we should fast, and we may even need to spend a night without sleep in order to pray through. If we pray in this way, we will see how much the Lord will come in. We should not forget how the disciples came to the Lord concerning an epileptic demon, asking, "Why were we not able to cast it out?" The Lord answered, "This kind does not go out except by prayer and fasting" (Matt. 17:19, 21).

Prayer is not simple. In this universe there is not only the physical world; there is also a spiritual world. Evil spiritual forces are always fighting, hindering, and frustrating the Lord's work. We must have prayer to face the situation and fight the battle. We cannot build up a church merely by teaching doctrines. Even in gospel preaching, we cannot merely preach to bring people to the Lord. We need to pray to fight the battle against the wiles of the strong man so that the Lord will bind the strong man and all the souls in his hand will be released. This can be carried out only by prevailing prayer, not by teaching or preaching alone.

May we all be impressed with this. This message is not merely a lesson in a classroom. Rather, this is a spiritual training for us to learn the way of the Lord. I look to the Lord concerning this, and I declare that my heart is absolutely with the Lord concerning this matter. May the Lord impress us, more than with any other matter, that we must go to Him to pray for the practice of the church life.

Chapter Six

THE SPIRITUAL WARFARE OF THE CHURCH

Scripture Reading: Eph. 6:10-20; Ezek. 37:1-10

THE DIVINE COMMISSION OF THE CHURCH

In this chapter we will see something concerning the spiritual warfare of the church. The creation of man was for two purposes. On the positive side, it was so that man would express God, and on the negative side, it was to deal with the enemy of God. This refers to the image of God and the authority of God. In the New Testament, especially in Ephesians, the book most related to the church, we can see the image and authority of God, that is, the way to express God corporately and fight the battle against the enemy of God in a corporate way. Nearly all the teachings in the New Testament are composed with the elements of the image of God to express God in Christ through the Spirit and the authority to fight the battle and deal with God's enemy. These are the two main components of God's eternal plan, and these are the two main items of the entire teaching of the Scriptures, especially in the New Testament.

In Ephesians, we can see the image of God especially in 4:22-24 which tells us to put off the old man and put on the new man, the corporate new creation in Christ, which was created according to the image of the Creator, that is, of God Himself. The church as the new creation has the image of God in order to express God in Christ through the Holy Spirit. Then in the last chapter of Ephesians, there is the fighting, the wrestling, the spiritual warfare to deal with the evil forces in the kingdom of darkness, that is, to deal with the enemy of God. If we are the victorious church, if we realize the real church life, then the Lord will be expressed through us that we may have His true image and the heavenly authority to fight the spiritual warfare to deal with the enemy of God.

The two aspects of the divine commission of the church are to express God in Christ through the Spirit and to deal with the enemy of God. The purpose of the messages in this book is not to help us merely to know some truths, doctrines, or teachings. Rather, it is to help us to realize the genuine life of a Christian, which is the real life of the church, the victorious, corporate life of the Body, in order to express Christ and to deal with the enemy of God. We must bring Christ to people, exhibit Christ, glorify Christ, and express Christ in the divine image. This is on the positive side. We also have to fight the battle, deal with the enemy, bind the strong man, and chase the forces of darkness. This is on the negative side. This is the divine commission committed by the Lord to the church. What are we here for? We are here for the exhibition and expression of Christ, on the positive side, and the fighting of the spiritual warfare to deal with the enemy of God on the negative side.

If we read Ephesians again with this point of view, we will see that the entire book can be summarized by these two aspects. The church is the Body of Christ to express and exhibit Christ and to glorify Christ in the divine image, and the church also fights the battle to bring the coming kingdom, to deal with the enemy of God, and to chase away the evil forces of darkness.

SPIRITUAL WARFARE BEING A CORPORATE MATTER

Ephesians 6:10-20 is the clearest portion of the New Testament dealing with spiritual warfare. Spiritual warfare is not an individual matter. Many of us received help from *The Pilgrim's Progress* when we were young, but the author of that book, John Bunyan, made spiritual warfare to be an individual matter. This may cause people to believe that the warrior in Ephesians 6 is an individual believer. In actuality, the warrior here is a corporate warrior, just as the Body in chapter one, the new man, the house of God, and the building in chapter two, the church as the mystery of Christ in chapter three, the Body and the new man in chapter four, and the bride as the wife in chapter five are all corporate. All these are not individual persons but a corporate person, which is the church. The church is the corporate Body of Christ, the corporate new man, the corporate building, the corporate mystery, the corporate wife, and the corporate warrior. Therefore, spiritual warfare is not a matter of the individual saint; it is a matter of the church. If we do not have the church life, we have lost the ground for spiritual warfare. If we are not in the reality of the Body life, we have no ground to fight the battle; we have been defeated already. Without the church life, we are defeated, and it is impossible for a defeated person to fight the enemy.

The ground and standing for us to fight the enemy is the church, and the church is in Christ, in the Spirit, and in the heavenlies. On the one hand, as long as someone is saved, he is in Christ, even if he is a defeated Christian. However, if he is not in the reality of the Body life, he is not in Christ practically and according to experience. Therefore, in order to fight the spiritual warfare, we must realize the church life.

We may declare, "We are not on the earth; we are in the heavenlies!" Whenever we are even a little earthly, we are defeated. We need to keep our heavenly ground and standing, but we must realize that the heavenly ground is for the Body corporately, not the members separately.

In the military today, it is foolish for a soldier to fight alone. In order to fight the battle, we must form an army. If there is no formation of the army, there is no possibility to fight the battle. In Ezekiel 37, when the dead bones were revived and made alive, they joined together. When they were dead, they were scattered in thorough, absolute death, but when they were made alive, they became members joined to be a living body. According to the context of the chapter, this living body is the house of Jehovah, the building, the dwelling place of God, and it is also the army. This body is the building and the army. This is a good picture of the Body life. Can separated and scattered bones fight the battle? This is ludicrous. We must realize that no matter how strong we feel, we are not adequate by ourselves to fight the battle. To fight the battle is a matter of the Body. We must be built together. We must be in oneness and harmony as the living Body, the living building, and the living house of God. Then we can be the army.

If we read Ephesians from the first chapter to the sixth chapter, we will see that warfare is a matter of the Body of Christ, and the Body is a new creation in Christ, in the Spirit, and in the heavenlies. First we must have the Body life, and then we can have the spiritual warfare. If we do not have the Body life, we are simply not adequate to have the warfare. In order to fight the battle, we must be in the reality of the Body life. In order to fight for America, one must be in the American armed forces. He cannot go to the battlefield alone. No one would be so foolish as to do this. He must first join the army and be trained, built up, and formed with the army. It is exactly the same with the Body of Christ. Why is spiritual warfare in the last chapter of Ephesians and not in the first, the second, or even the fifth chapter? It is because warfare is something of the Body, which is in Christ, in the Spirit, and in the heavenly places.

SPIRITUAL WARFARE BEING
AGAINST THE EVIL SPIRITUAL FORCES

We also must realize that spiritual warfare is not a fighting against humans, that is, against flesh and blood. Rather, we fight with the spiritual forces, the evil spirits. This is not a small matter. I still remember well how Brother Watchman Nee held a conference in 1928 in which he spoke about the spiritual warfare in a very practical and detailed way. He was very much attacked by the enemy for this. After a certain period of time he told me, "Brother, if we are going to talk about spiritual warfare and deal with it in a practical way, we need at least thirty brothers and sisters to pray for us day and night. Otherwise, there will be many attacks." Therefore, may the Lord cover us with His blood! The evil spiritual forces are not merely a doctrine or a term. In the universe there is such an evil force, which is the kingdom of darkness, the evil spirits. Even today we may not realize how much the evil spirits are working to damage the kingdom of God in order to frustrate the fulfillment of God's purpose. This is a real fighting. Therefore, we do not fight with flesh and blood. We fight with the evil spirits. Our enemy is not people; our enemy is the forces of darkness.

In the past years and even up until today, it is difficult to say how many rumors the enemy has been constantly spreading. In 2 Corinthians 6:8 the apostle Paul speaks of "evil report and good report." Even the apostle suffered many evil reports. The evil reports are simply rumors. I do not have the time or the heart to speak in detail, but it is a fact that there has been rumor after rumor constantly against us. Whenever one is in the lead, he is exposed to attack to some degree, and the attack of the enemy is upon him. When we were in mainland China, Brother Nee was very exposed to attack because he was taking the lead. I was very close to him, and nearly day by day I saw many things. As early as 1934 I was brought into this fighting because from that time on I began to share the responsibility to deal with this warfare. I saw the wiles, the tactics, and the subtle ways of the enemy and how our brother was attacked very much. The most serious attacks were the rumors.

There is such a reality that in this universe there are the evil forces of darkness, the evil spirits, fighting, frustrating, and damaging the interests of the Lord's kingdom and His testimony. What shall we do? Shall we consider those who have been utilized by the enemy to spread rumors as our enemy? If we do this, we are wrong. The real enemy is not the people. The real enemy is the evil forces behind the people. The people are merely the puppets of the enemy to be utilized by him. We should not fight the people; we should fight the evil forces behind them. The way to fight the evil forces is not by the flesh but by the Spirit, in the Spirit, and by prayer. The only way we can deal with the enemy who is working, fighting, behind certain people is to pray, to appeal to the throne in the heavens as the highest authority. Therefore, there is the need for real and prevailing corporate prayer. The church needs to come together to pray, not to deal with people. I have learned the lesson that whenever there is a rumor, we should not deal with it directly. When there is a rumor about the church, we should not talk to people or explain things to them. The more we explain, the more the rumors will come out. We should simply go to the Lord and appeal to the highest authority. Through the throne we deal with the evil forces which are behind the blood and flesh. We must learn this and practice this.

THE WHOLE ARMOR OF GOD

Being Girded with Truth

Most of the items of the divine armor of God in Ephesians 6 are for protection. First, we must gird our loins with truth (v. 14a). Truth here does not refer to the doctrine of the word of God, because the word is related to the sword in verse 17. Truth refers to faithfulness, sincerity, and reality. When we practice the church life, we must be real. I must be real to you, and you must be real to me. There must be no falsehood and no pretense. If we have pretense and falsehood, we do not have truth among us; that is, we are not real. A Chinese proverb says, "To have a pretense is to stand on melting ice." In the church life, everything we do and speak must be real. Otherwise, we should not do it or speak it. If we love a brother, we should love in reality. If we do not love, we should not love in pretense. To pretend to love without real love is false. This causes us to lose the ground to fight the battle because the evil spirits will attack our conscience. The evil spirits know where we are, what we are, and what is in our hearts. Therefore, we must be real, not only before God but also before the enemy. Then we will have the ground to fight the battle.

Verse 14 speaks of being girded with truth. To be girded is to be strengthened. If we do not have truth, but rather everything in the church is false, we lose our girding up, and we can never be strengthened. A soldier must be girded up in order to be strong to fight. If we do not have truth but are pretending and false, not speaking real things or doing real things, we are finished; we cannot fight the battle.

In order to maintain truth, sincerity, faithfulness, and reality among the saints, we must do everything in a real way. We must do nothing in a pretending way. We must hate pretense. I am sorry for the situation among many Christians today. Even some of the spiritual persons play politics. They may speak well to a brother, but an hour later they may speak evilly about him to someone else. This is politics. If we want to realize the church by the grace and mercy of God, we must speak truthfully and faithfully to the brothers. We may say to one, "Brother, in this matter I do not agree with you. I feel you are wrong." However, we must say this in the spirit and not in the flesh. If we are not able to say it in the spirit, we should not say it at all, but we should not pretend. We should not tell a brother that nothing is wrong and then turn around and say something different to someone else. This is falsehood. It makes the church false and not real. Then the church loses the ground to fight the battle.

We are defeated already if we speak lies to one another. If you pretend to love me, and I pretend to be nice to you, we have already been defeated by the enemy. How then can we fight the battle? We must be sincere to the saints. If we realize that a brother is unable to receive a word from us at the present time, or if we do not feel that we are fully in the spirit, we should not say anything. Do not play politics; do not be political among the Lord's children. Of course, we should not lose our temper. We should not be angry with people, but we should be genuine.

The Breastplate of Righteousness

We also need the breastplate of righteousness (v. 14b). We must be righteous; we cannot be unrighteous. If we lose our righteousness, we lose the ground to fight the spiritual battle. If we lie to one another, for example, there is falsehood and unrighteousness among us. Righteousness must be maintained among the saints in the church. Otherwise, the enemy will take the unrighteousness in the church as the weak point to attack. This is why we must deal with all unrighteous things in order to maintain the righteousness in the church. If we do not have righteousness, we do not have protection for our breast. This has much to do with the conscience. We need righteousness as a breastplate to protect our conscience. If we do not have righteousness as a covering, there will be attacks on our conscience.

Being Shod with the Gospel of Peace

Verse 15 speaks of having our feet shod with the firm foundation of the gospel of peace. Here the gospel is likened to a pair of shoes. When we walk, we touch the earth, and there are many things that can make our feet dirty or hurt them. Therefore, we need a pair of good shoes to protect our feet from being dirtied and hurt by the touch with the earth. What are the Christian's shoes? The Christian's shoes are the preaching of the gospel. The gospel is a good pair of shoes to protect our Christian "feet" from being dirtied and hurt by the earthly touch. Therefore, we need to preach the gospel. Wherever we go, we should tell people that we are Christians and that they must believe into Christ Jesus as the Lord. If we do this, we will be protected. We must have some outreach through gospel preaching. This is a protection to us.

The Shield of Faith

The shield of faith quenches all the flaming darts of the evil one (v. 16). Most of these darts are doubts. We should give up all our doubts, not only about God, but even about the believers, the brothers and sisters. The enemy constantly sends darts to make us doubt others. If we accept the darts of doubting, we will have problems with the brothers. We must always keep faith as our protection from the attack of the enemy's darts.

The Helmet of Salvation

The helmet of salvation is for our head (v. 17a). As we realize the church life and fight the battle, we always need to pray that the Lord will cover our head. The Lord must cover our head with His precious and victorious blood. Our head needs the covering because the head has much to do with the mind, the way of thinking. There are always the openings for the enemy to come in to attack us through the mind, the mentality. If the saints come together for only a few weeks, they will feel good toward one another, but gradually over the months and years suspicions may grow between them. We cannot say why, but the saints become suspicious without any reason. This is one example of the attack from the enemy. Other kinds of thoughts also come as darts from the enemy. Therefore, we need our head covered. We must pray that the Lord will cover our head, our mentality, our thinking, our mind. We need the helmet of salvation.

The Sword of the Spirit

In addition to the above items, there are two weapons. The first is to exercise to contact the word by the Spirit (v. 17b). We must read the word prayerfully so it may be living, powerful, and prevailing to us. We should take the word not in dead letters but in living power. We can exercise the word as the living sword to attack the enemy. This is our offensive weapon.

All Prayer and Petition

The last item of the armor is the most important. This is prayer (vv. 18-19). This is not merely to pray for our small personal matters. Many good saints pray day by day only for their small matters, such as their house and pets. A certain elderly sister in my hometown prayed much for the chickens she raised. She prayed that the Lord would protect the chickens and the things she needed to raise them. We should forget all such matters related to our family and our living. The Lord told us that our Father knows everything that we need. Rather, we should pray for the kingdom, the gospel, the church, and the Lord's interest.

Verse 18 says, "By means of all prayer and petition, praying at every time in spirit and watching unto this in all perseverance and petition concerning all the saints." *Prayer* is a general term, while to petition is to pray in a specific way with a certain purpose. Verses 19-20 continue, "And for me, that utterance may be given to me in the opening of my mouth, to make known in boldness the mystery of the gospel, for which I am an ambassador in a chain, that in it I would speak boldly, as I ought to speak." *Me* in verse 19 refers to the apostle, the sent one. *Utterance* here is the Greek word *logos,* meaning word. Our utterance is the proper, expressive word. These verses indicate that the things we must pray for are the kingdom of God, the saints of God, the gospel of the Lord, and the Lord's interest. If, for example, we see certain things in the church, we should not talk to one another as if reporting news, providing material to gossip about. To gossip about church affairs opens the door for the enemy to come in and attack the church. The more we know something about the church, the more we need to bring it to the Lord, to touch the throne by our prevailing prayer. This is the right way to pray. If we are properly realizing the church life, we will stop all gossiping and be prevailing, living, active, and positive in prayer. We will go to the Lord to pray, to touch the throne, and to bring all problems to the throne.

We intend to practice the real church life, but there are many things involved with this. Therefore, we must give up gossiping and common talking and be positive and active in prayer. We should go to the Lord and pray by ourselves and with two or more others. We must take the ground and standing of the church, identify with the heavenly Head, and pray in a prevailing way for the church. If we see a weakness with someone, we must not talk. If we see that some of the leading ones are not adequate or qualified, we must not criticize. Rather, we should go to the Head on the throne and pray. Then the Lord will solve the problem or remove it.

We must not point to someone and say, "What kind of a leading one or elder is that?" When we criticize in this way, we damage the church life and open the way for the enemy to come in and attack the church and bring death into the Body. We are defeated by the enemy already. We lose our ground, and we damage the church very much. The only thing we must do is to bring this matter to the Head and pray, "Lord, be merciful to us and be merciful to that brother. Lord, we leave it to You what You must do." The Lord will honor our prayer. By praying in this way, we will be those standing in the opening to shut the way for the enemy to come in to attack and damage the Body. We must simply go to the Lord and pray. If someone else has the same realization we have, we should be one to go to the Lord to pray. Our weapon is our prayer for the matters we see and for the Lord's servants.

We must take the ground of being in the church, in Christ, in the Spirit, and in the heavenlies. Moreover, we are not dealing with mere humans; we are dealing with the evil forces of darkness, the kingdom of the enemy. This is our real enemy. We must also remember our defenses: being girded with truth, having the breastplate of righteousness, being shod with the gospel, having the shield of faith, and putting on the helmet of salvation. We must also learn how to exercise in the word in the spirit in a living way, and we must learn how to pray and petition. Many times we must pray with all kinds of prayer and petition.

The church life is a prayer life. I especially ask the leading ones among the saints to realize a real prayer life. The leading brothers must come together to pray often and pray more. Then they will help all the saints to learn to have a prayer life. To simply have a prayer meeting in the church once a week is not sufficient. The church must have a prayer life, and the leading ones must take the lead in this prayer life. All these items are the armor we need to fight the battle. In these days the battle is not a small matter. It is not a small matter to speak about the eternal purpose and central thought of God, the church life, the testimony, and the recovery of the testimony. We cannot succeed merely by speaking or preaching. We must realize these matters by fighting and by praying.

Here are many lessons for us to learn. If the Lord is gracious to us that we may learn the lessons of realizing the Body life and the real spiritual warfare, there is no need for other teachings. This is sufficient. By this we will be exercised, disciplined, ruled, and controlled by the Lord in the spirit. We will learn all the lessons spontaneously, and there will be no need for others to teach and direct us; we will be directed already. This is the only way for us to realize the church life and have a real recovery of the Lord's testimony on this earth, especially in this country, in these last days. This is why I am so burdened for these matters, and this is why I have kept these matters for the end of these messages.

I am waiting to see what will come of these lessons. Let us pray and look to the Lord that He will make them so real to us, so that each one of us may realize the church life and realize the real spiritual warfare for the kingdom of the Lord.